T0369995

RANDOM HOUSE
LARGE
PRINT

The Next Conversation

The Next Conversation

Argue Less, Talk More

Jefferson Fisher

RANDOM HOUSE LARGE PRINT

Published by Random House Large Print in association with TarcherPerigee, an imprint of Penguin Random House LLC, 1745 Broadway, New York, NY 10019, penguinrandomhouse.com

Original cover design: Pete Garceau
Design adapted for Large Print

The Library of Congress has established a Cataloging-in-Publication record for this title.

FIRST LARGE PRINT EDITION

ISBN: 979-8-217-06762-6

Printed in the United States of America

2nd Printing

The authorized representative in the EU for product safety and compliance is Penguin Random House Ireland, Morrison Chambers, 32 Nassau Street, Dublin D02 YH68, Ireland, https://eu-contact.penguin.ie.

For

Sierra, who supports me
Jett and Ruby, who inspire me
My siblings, who inspired me first
My parents, who prayed over me
And all who tried that and followed me

There ain't no good guy.
There ain't no bad guy.
There's only you and me and we
just disagree.

—Dave Mason, "We Just Disagree"

CONTENTS

The Next Conversation

Prologue

The worn-out Berber carpet of the old ranch house felt scratchy on my legs. Wearing an oversize shirt and my Spider-Man underwear, I curled up into a ball in the corner of the main room. My hair and skin were still wet from my rushed, unheated shower. I was shivering. I was also grinning ear-to-ear.

Eight-year-old me wasn't going to miss a thing.

Everyone was in the main room. The patriarch of the family was my great-grandfather, who was a federal judge. My grandfather, father, first cousins, great uncles—you name it—were all trial lawyers. Every year, the Fisher men would get together for an opening-weekend hunt in the Hill Country of West Texas. There were thirteen joining in total, and for the first time, I made it fourteen. I felt like I had been called up to the big leagues. Me—finally old enough to go on an eight-hour drive with my dad listening to James Taylor, Jim Croce, and Jerry

Jeff Walker. Me—finally old enough to be around the big boys. I hardly spoke a word, mind you, but it didn't matter. I drank IBC Root Beer and ate more beef jerky than my momma would ever have allowed.

The first night was an experience cemented into my memory.

As dinner finished, my grandfather put his plate down and scooted to the edge of his couch seat. He began to tell a story. Something about his job, a judge, and a courthouse. I immediately recognized it as the same story he had told my dad earlier that day while we were fixing an old deer blind. Earlier, though, the story was more matter-of-fact. His voice came out plain as he told it while searching for green paint in his truck bed.

But this was special. It was the same words, but it was a very different story.

I was entranced, watching as he stood up to reenact a scene. He used his hands and face to give texture to his voice. His volume went up on the exciting parts, low and slow on the intense parts. Even his tone changed. Could this be the same story? He captivated the room for nearly ten minutes. After a long pause, he delivered the punch line, and the room filled with laughter. I felt as though I had seen a magic show.

The end of his story opened the floor to others as one by one my cousins, dad, and even my great-grandfather took turns with courtroom stories of their own. As trial lawyers, they were all wonderful storytellers. The laughter went on for hours into the night.

I sat there in that corner transfixed by every story, every word, with my knees tucked into my sleep shirt. I took it all in until I fell asleep. It was late. My dad carried me off to bed, beef jerky still in my hand.

The whole evening for me had been the discovery of something new yet strangely familiar, as if I had seen it all before. I remember it immediately felt right to me, like a shoe that fit the first time you tried it on.

That night, and for the next ten years of opening weekends, I received my family's inheritance: a passed-on identity dedicated to advocacy through storytelling. I realized with each year gone by that law was only the family profession—communication was the true family passion.

To no one's surprise, I wanted to go to law school and become a trial lawyer.

And after practicing for ten years, I still don't know of another profession like it. I get hired to handle problems with people I personally don't have problems with. What's more, the opposing party also has their own lawyer, who's getting paid to have problems with me. Every day, I go up against people whose primary job is to make sure that I lose. When it comes to a jury trial, the stakes can't be any higher. How I communicate, and how I teach my client to communicate, can mean the difference between recovering their livelihood and losing it forever. Each case is a new lesson, whether I'm deposing witnesses, cross-examining parties, or giving arguments before a judge or jury. My entire purpose is to run toward conflict.

If you're inclined to believe that I learned my communication skills in law school, don't. Law school teaches you how to apply the law: principles of contracts, torts, constitutional law, and state and federal rules of procedure—all important. But you won't sit in a class on how to speak to each other with empathy. You won't hear a lesson on how to defuse a heated argument. Law school teaches you how to read the law. It doesn't teach you how to read people.

I had to learn that part myself.

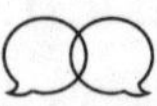

"Do you yike it?!" my sister, Sarah, squealed through her pacifier as she brought me the fifth round of invisible pancakes. As the oldest of four, I loved being the big brother.

By the time I was thirteen, my bond with my siblings was so strong that they obeyed me almost better than they did my parents. I was like a mother hen wherever we went. And by the time I was sixteen, I was driving them to school while going over their spelling words.

To be clear, my parents are loving and wonderful. I was only as good as I was because they poured so much of themselves into me those first four years before my sister was born. I also just truly enjoyed the responsibility of being the big brother.

Being the oldest supposedly leads to more emotional stability, initiative, and the like. But for me, it taught me to hone communication fundamentals at an early age.

I quickly learned to acknowledge Sarah by pretending to gobble up the invisible food while smiling and saying, "Mm-hmm, delicious." I found that words of kindness worked better at getting her to open up than words of anger. My younger brother Jonathan would say my name repeatedly (they call me Bubba, a southern term of endearment for the eldest boy) and stammer until he got his sentences out. I learned that if I patiently waited and repeated his words back to him while nodding my head, he felt understood. He also couldn't say his consonants for a long time, only vowels. I naturally became his interpreter, identifying nonverbal mannerisms and foreseeing situations that would frustrate him before they happened. Jacob, my youngest brother, was the most emotionally intense of the three. He felt his emotions big, quickly losing his temper. I figured out that if I slowed my words and lowered my voice, so would he. I learned to let him feel his feelings without me taking them personally. That sometimes a hug said more than any words I could say. Each sibling had a unique personality that took a special approach, a special touch to connect with them on a deeper level.

One of the most critical skills that I developed as the oldest was my ability to mediate and resolve conflict. If two of my siblings began arguing over our sister's Polly Pocket, I'd quickly stop the yelling, have them each give their side of the story, and then make the judgment call on whose turn it was and what the compromise would be. And it worked. I became proficient at teaching my siblings how to communicate their needs and understand the needs of one another. Serving as the role model for communication between my siblings was daily life.

Now married with two kids, it's still daily life. I've been the communicator in every phase, every relationship, every friend group. Maybe you think it's just a knack for talking. I know it to be something more. Every night as I was growing up, my dad sat on the edge of my bed, leaned over, and whispered, "Dear God, give Jefferson wisdom and always be his friend." I believe in the power of prayer. And I believe that without my parents' prayer, you wouldn't be reading this book.

In 2020, I made partner at a prestigious defense firm. But despite this achievement, I was professionally depressed. I always came back to the same metaphor: I felt like I was running with a parachute. I was billing and working cases, yes, but creatively, I was getting nowhere.

To make things harder, my dad worked at the same firm. When I first told him I had thoughts of going off on my own, let's just say it didn't go well. Honestly, it didn't go well for the next twenty conversations and even up to when I announced it to the firm. He fought for me to stay. Those were hard talks.

I did two things in January 2022 that would change everything.

First, I opened my own law firm, Fisher Firm, handling personal injury cases.

I didn't have an office or an assistant—heck, I didn't even have a printer. I surfed coffee shops with my laptop and borrowed friends' empty offices. I quickly signed up clients, and man, did it feel amazing. I got to help real people with real problems. I'd cut the parachute, and I was finally making up ground.

Second, I made my first social media post giving communication advice.

Originally, I wanted to use it to generate leads. I saw so many lawyers posting on social media doing the only thing they knew: selling. They saw it as the new billboard frontier, telling people what to do and who to call after an accident. I even tried some of it myself. But afterward, it just didn't feel right. My mind flashed to those attorneys whose faces are splattered on billboards, seen holding hammers, flamethrowers, and boxing gloves, saying outrageous things like "Have you been injured? I'm the Texas Cheese Grater! Call me and get that cheddar now!" Blerf. I shuddered. I can't stand that stuff. Most of all, that wasn't me.

I chose a different path. Instead of selling myself, I would provide value for free. Not about what would benefit me, but about what would benefit other people. And this time, I would do it being authentically me, the person I've been all along. Jefferson.

How could I truly help people?

It needed to be something relatable, a message of light and good into people's homes and workplaces. My mind flashed back to my parents' question to me whenever I didn't know what to say to someone: "Well, what do you want them to know?" The answer hit me like a ton of bricks. I'd tell them what I know better than anyone else I knew. I'd help them learn how to communicate.

I didn't have a cool desk setup or a studio to record in with a fancy camera, but I had my truck and my phone. That'd have to do. I turned my phone selfie-style and pressed record. I decided on the fly that it would be "How to argue like a lawyer pt.1" and that I'd boil it down to three easy points. In the front seat of my empty truck, I talked to the screen of my phone about how to keep your questions shorter, how to be less emotionally reactive, and how too much cursing was like over-seasoning your food. I'd run across something previously that said that a video needed to have a **call to action**. So, at the end of the video, I said, "Try that and follow me." For whatever reason, I couldn't tell you why, I put my hand up to my mouth at the last second when I said it. I decided to roll with it. I took a big gulp and posted the forty-seven-second clip to social media.

I didn't expect anything to happen. So far, all my videos had zero views. In fact, I'd even googled "Why do my videos have 0 views?" and "How do I make a reel?"

What happened next was nothing I was prepared for. After an hour passed, my "how to argue" video started ramping up in views, quickly reaching into the thousands. The next day, it was in the millions. I didn't realize, of course, that it would also mean that millions of people would see my daughter's pink car seat and my son's sippy cup in the back, along with my thoughtless fashion choice—an unstructured polo with a suit jacket. Who gets dressed thinking they're going to be seen by millions of people that day?

People didn't seem to care. It was where I was in my life. It made them feel like I was speaking directly to them, with no upsell, no gimmicks. It was real.

"What do I do now?" I asked a friend. She replied, "You make more."

So I did.

That year, I gained more than five million social media followers, including hundreds of celebrities and public figures, all while using my iPhone from my driver's seat to give communication advice. Always the same way—alone, in my car, wherever I could park between leaving the law firm and arriving home. Never scripted, always posted on the same day that I filmed. No video editor or fancy graphics or trendy captions. Just me, holding my phone and being myself.

And despite doing everything alone in my car, I soon found myself in front of thousands of real people giving keynotes at conferences and speaking to organizations asking to learn from my communication techniques. I even spoke at NASA. Every time I spoke, all I could think was, "What are all y'all doing here?" I reached 250,000 email subscribers wanting my weekly communication tip, and I signed a book deal with Penguin Random House to start writing the book you're holding now. I launched **The Jefferson Fisher Podcast**, which shot straight to the top of the charts and is the number one communication podcast in the world. I've also grown an amazing online community filled with resources and classes that equip people with practical ways to improve their communication. My videos have received over half a billion views across all platforms. I'm blessed and humbled to have received some of the kindest, most thoughtful daily messages of thanks and gratitude. I can't believe I get to help others in this way, much less that I'm typing these words.

I still practice law every day, now helping people from all over the US with their personal injuries and connecting them to attorneys I trust. I still record a short video every day. I still say, "Try that and follow me." Millions have tried it and followed me. I say that from a deep place of gratitude.

I never dreamed this is where it would go.

But the dreams didn't stop there.

Five months after I opened Fisher Firm, my dad left his firm of thirty-five years to join me, his son, for no other reason than simply for us to practice law together. "You still got room for the old man?" he asked with a smile. I was speechless. There was nothing I could've ever wanted more. My eyes still well up with happy tears now as I write about it.

Introduction

Not long after uploading my first video, I started to receive messages—thousands of them. So many that there was no way I could read, let alone respond to, all of them. The messages were from followers of my content asking me for advice.

They weren't asking for my guidance on big philosophical questions about religion or politics, or even legal stuff. They wanted my advice on the day-to-day, micro moments about real things that real people struggle with, everything from mundane issues to stories that'll rip your heart out.

- What do I say to a superior who always puts down my ideas?
- What do I say to my adult daughter who I haven't seen in years?

- What do I say to my partner, who always has to be right?

After thousands of messages like these, the one thing I've learned is that no matter how they frame the question, their problem isn't **what** to say—it's **how** to say it.

Whenever I get one of these questions, the first thing I ask is what my parents always asked me: "Well, what do you want them to know?" So far, I've never received back, "I don't know." I always get a quick answer. People already know what they want to say, because deep down, it's a reflection of what they're already feeling: **I want them to know it hurts me. I want them to know I need space. I want them to know why I'm upset.** The feelings reveal themselves naturally. But articulating those feelings to another person? Not so easy.

It's deflating, really, how something so simple can feel so out of reach.

If you picked up this book, chances are you're reaching for the same thing: real solutions for real problems. You don't need the **what**, you need the **how**. How do you express yourself in a way that respects both your perspective and the perspective of the other person? How do you stand up for yourself without losing the relationship? How do you voice your thoughts with authenticity and empathy but still show that you have a backbone?

The easy answer you're looking for is connection.

The more honest answer you deserve is in the pages that lie ahead.

Why I Wrote This Book

I wrote this book for three reasons:

1. Because my social media followers asked for it. To me, it's their book.
2. To teach you what I know that will improve your next conversation.
3. To preserve a piece of me for my kids and my family.

Before you crack into it, I need you to understand something important. The communication skills in this book aren't borrowed principles. Outside of a few studies and commentary from other scientific fields—psychology, neuroscience, behavioral science—you won't be seeing many sources. What you're about to read is knowledge collected from my life experiences and how I communicate.

I am not a therapist. I am not a psychologist. If anything I say in this book somehow conflicts in some way with one of these specialists, believe them over me. I'm not going to ask you to identify your attachment style or encourage you to take a quiz to find out which conflict personality you have. If you're looking to take a deep dive into the latest statistics or a case study about how the social dynamic patterns of bees can help you communicate, I'm not the guy for you.

What I've written are lessons from my daily grind in the real-world trenches of arguments, disagreements, heated debates, and difficult conversations.

What I offer is down-to-earth, homegrown advice outside of the textbooks and lectures.

And maybe that's just what more of the world needs.

How This Book Will Help You

While I am a trial lawyer, you won't find a speck of law in what you're about to read. This book isn't about my profession, or even about lawyers.

It's about how to speak boldly, with your chin up, to embrace the vulnerability that comes with laying all your cards on the table.

How to say what you mean and mean what you say.

It's about choosing courage over comfort, even when your voice shakes.

Speaking directly doesn't mean you lack empathy or consideration for the other person's feelings. Being direct means that you have the self-assurance that you can respect the other person, as well as yourself, enough to communicate your needs openly without fear.

You don't have to be an assertive person to speak

assertively. The words do it for you. That's what this book will give you: the words.

In this book, you'll get answers to questions that so many people wrestle with:

- How do I talk to someone who's defensive?
- What do I say when someone belittles me?
- How do I assert my boundaries?

To get you there, I've broken it down into two parts. Part one tells you how to first connect with yourself. That sounds woo-woo, I know. But it's not. It's about where to go in your mind when conflict appears, and most important, how to **leverage** the mindset for better outcomes. Part two teaches you how to use that leverage to connect with other people. How you connect looks different based on context, whether it's working through a difficult conversation or needing to stand up for yourself. Whatever context you find yourself in, I've created three rules that will build the connection for you:

1. Say it with control.
2. Say it with confidence.
3. Say it to connect.

Behind each rule are proven tactics you can use immediately. Throughout this book, I'll show you what confident communication looks, sounds, and feels like. You'll learn from real-life stories from my personal and professional experiences. You'll also see yourself in hypothetical conversations that hit close to home. You'll learn what to say and what not to say, and of course, how to say it.

After reading the pages ahead, you're going to be able to remove the difficult from difficult conversations, making space for more **real** in your life. Real friendships, real connection, and real growth. And I don't just mean at home or in relationships. You'll find the real you starting to show up at work and in meetings. You'll respond to texts and emails differently. People will know where you stand. You'll watch your confidence turn into credibility—and that, I can't wait to see.

How to Apply This Book

While reading this book or watching any of my videos, you may ask: How will I remember all this when I need it?

My answer is simple: you won't. You can't read everything and expect to immediately apply everything. That's too much at once, like trying to drink from a firehose. You'll set yourself up for failure.

Instead, pick one.

Pick one tip that resonates with you and apply it as soon as you can. For example, let's say the lesson that hits home with you is the one about overapologizing, in chapter seven. Focus on that one lesson. Find ways to keep it close to your thoughts, like writing it down somewhere you can see, saying it out loud to yourself, or telling a close friend who can keep you accountable. Then, start using it. Catch yourself every time you give a needless "sorry" and edit it out of every sentence you say, email you type, or message you text.

Commit yourself to that one rule. Then, and only then, when you can go a week without a single unnecessary apology, should you move on to another lesson that also resonates with you.

This book includes tips I've handpicked, from my most popular and viral videos to exclusive takeaways I've never shared before. If you're reading this because you follow me on social media, hi, it's still me. I'm proud to finally give you something tangible to mark up, tear up, and make yours. I know you'll find it worth the wait. It's time to say more of what you mean and mean more of what you say. It's time to communicate your needs openly without fear.

So come hop in to the passenger seat, and I'll bring the IBC Root Beer and beef jerky. You're well on your way to making your next conversation the one that changes everything.

PART I

The Essentials

I don't need to convince you that communication matters. You know that. What I do need to persuade you of, however, is the reach of it.

Your words have a ripple effect.

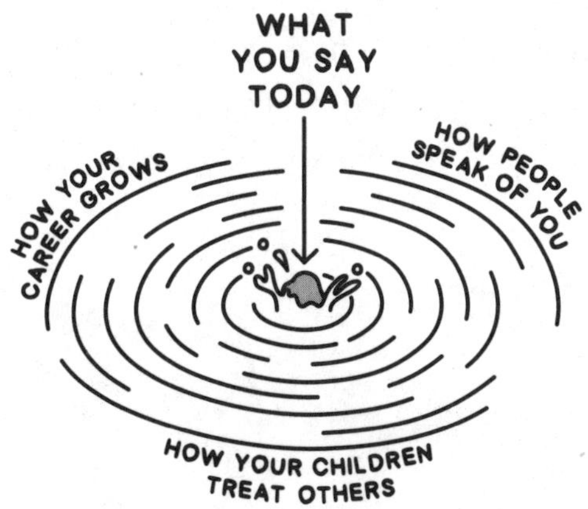

It doesn't matter how insignificant you think you are—whether you think you're a somebody or a nobody, your words have power beyond anything you'll live to see.

How you talk to your coworker, or the person behind the counter, affects how they talk to their friends and their family when they go home. How you talk to your kids affects how they will talk to their kids. Your words don't just matter now. They matter to generations of people you'll never meet. People you'll never know exist. The right sentence to the right person can change lives.

Yes, actions can speak louder than words, but they're not a replacement for them. You can't call yourself a kind person if you don't use kind words.

Who do your words say you are?

The ripples keep going long after the rock hits the water.

What you'll learn in The Essentials is a mindset that prepares you to create waves of positive impact that will resonate through your relationships to last a lifetime, and many times over.

CHAPTER 1

Never Win an Argument

I don't trust you as far as I can throw you!" he bellowed.

In all honesty, it was a compliment. He could've thrown me pretty far.

In his tan coveralls with a white oval patch that had "LaPray" embroidered in black on the upper left pocket, Bobby LaPray glared at me with enough heat to burn a hole through my suit jacket.

I generally don't know what someone looks like before I meet them at their deposition. Whatever I pictured Bobby LaPray looking like, it wasn't this. Sitting at the conference room table waiting for people to arrive, I looked up to see a half human, half giant. His outline took up the whole doorway. Naturally, I stood up and walked over to him to shake his hand and introduce myself.

"Jefferson Fisher," I said with a smile.

"Hmph. Bobby," he muttered.

Now, I'm not a small guy. I'm over six feet tall.

But I barely came up to Bobby LaPray's chest. He was an absolute mountain. As we shook hands, the squeeze from his ginormous callused hands left an imprint on mine like a scene from a Tom and Jerry cartoon. I'd never been around someone so physically intimidating.

The case involved a bar fight, and I was representing a bystander who had gotten caught up in the scuffle. As part of the case, I needed to depose Bobby LaPray, a witness to the events. In a deposition, I get the chance to ask people questions under oath, typically to learn what they know before they testify at trial.

Clockwise around the antique conference room table sat the court reporter writing everything down, Bobby LaPray, the opposing attorney, and me. After asking Bobby to raise his right hand and placing him under oath, the court reporter gave her customary nod for me to begin.

I asked Bobby LaPray routine questions about his background and what had led up to the fight. They were easy, open-ended questions: What time did you arrive? Who did you talk to first? Did you see so-and-so or do this-and-that? It's common to use such questions to build a chronology of the events from a witness's particular point of view. At all times, I made sure I was kind and polite—90 percent because that's my personality and 10 percent out of sheer self-preservation. He was not someone I wanted upset.

But no matter how many softball questions I asked, Bobby LaPray was becoming increasingly agitated. I had seen it enough times in my experience to know. His eyebrows began furrowing with each answer. A sign of negative emotion. His breathing got heavier as he switched from exhaling through his nose to exhaling through his mouth. A sign of increased stress. He started wringing his massive hands together as he spoke. A sign of anxiety.

It didn't matter what I did. It seemed as if just my existence in the room offended him. I could sense the tension around the table heightening the more displeased Bobby LaPray looked. Like I was blowing up a balloon and it was about to pop.

Finally, I asked him, "Mr. LaPray, would you like a break?"

The room went silent.

"No," Bobby LaPray said, clearing his throat. "But I got something to say."

His words rang out louder than necessary. So much so that the court reporter jumped. I quickly glanced at the other attorney, who couldn't have been younger than sixty-five. He looked more nervous than I was. When we locked eyes, he gave me a wide-eyed look and slowly shook his head as if to say, "If this goes south, you're on your own." I turned back to look at my witness.

"Yessir?" I inquired.

Bobby LaPray took a big breath in. "You can cut all this buddy-buddy stuff."

Except he didn't say "stuff."

"You lawyers are the worst thing to happen to America," he continued. "All you do is lie."

He slammed his hand on the table, then drew it upward with a pointed finger at me, saying, "So go on and ask me your stupid questions. Just know, I don't trust you as far as I can throw you! I'm tellin' you, lawyers are the worst thing to happen to this country," he repeated.

The court reporter gave an anxious look.

At that moment, a hundred thoughts raced through my mind.

First, I'm well accustomed to this derogatory stereotype of attorneys, especially personal injury attorneys. I try very hard to work against it, though it's a reputation that some attorneys, frankly, rightly deserve. So a put-down joke or snide remark about my profession is nothing new. I understood.

Second, I didn't blame him for not trusting me. Not because I was trying to mislead him, but because to his mind, I represented all the bad things he ever thought he knew or had heard of about the law, lawyers, and "the system." Of course he had no reason to trust me. I understood.

It was the "stupid questions" that got me.

I know good and well that I do many, many stupid things every day. But what I don't do is ask stupid questions.

In that instant, a wave of anger surged through

me. I felt my whole body go tense. My ears got hot as I shifted my weight in my seat. I could sense that I was becoming defensive. My questions up to that point had barely scratched the surface. Nothing about them had been difficult or even uncomfortable. **Stupid? I'll show him stupid**, I thought. I felt myself wanting to come back with quips about his size in relation to his intelligence. Just a few well-placed cutting words and I'd best him. I tried to tell myself that his reaction was all I needed to know about who he truly was.

But I'd been wrong before.

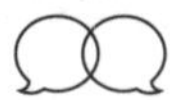

When I was in third grade, my school started a reading buddy program, pairing strong readers with those who hadn't learned yet. That's how I got paired with Evan. Twice a week, we'd sit on beanbags during our library period. I'd listen as he would struggle to read aloud books like **Brown Bear, Brown Bear, What Do You See?** by Bill Martin Jr.

Evan was physically much bigger than I was. Back then, I had a hard time understanding how he was so big but couldn't read. When he'd come across a word he didn't know, my job was to help him sound it out. But he still struggled. So I figured out ways to explain things to him differently, like associating words with memorable phrases or creating metaphors on the fly with whatever was near us in the room. I got good at crafting little tricks that engaged Evan's interests, making harder ideas more memorable.

Sometimes we'd do our reading sessions during our lunch period. While I'd pull out my lunch in a brown bag with a handwritten smiley face on it that my momma had made me that day, I'd watch as a teacher would bring him a tray from the cafeteria.

Evan's momma didn't make his lunch. I began to notice that his clothes never seemed to fit him, like they were three sizes too big.

Once, when we were going over **throw**, **threw**, and **through**, I tried to help by relating it to how he'd throw a ball to his dad.

Evan flatly replied, "I don't know who my dad is."

I vividly remember feeling as though I couldn't move my mouth. I was speechless. My heart broke for him. I'd later learn that Evan had been living with his grandparents. His dad had left shortly after he was born. His mom was in jail. But in third grade, I had no grasp of his reality. No clue about the true struggles he was facing. With two loving parents who read and told stories to me at night, I knew then that he was living in a world I knew nothing about.

As we continued over that fall semester and into the next year, Evan's reading level improved with each session until he was reading all on his own. I couldn't have been prouder. Exposure to Evan's inner struggles was another defining moment in my life at an early age. And it was a lesson I've never forgotten.

Zinging a put-down at ten-foot-tall Bobby wouldn't help anything. It would only hurt—if not the deposition, then most definitely my face. And besides, my client's case needed this information. **Put it down, Jefferson**, I said to myself. I let out a long, silent breath through my nose. As I dropped the tension in my shoulders, my thoughts of retaliation faded.

What I became more curious about, however, was the disproportionality of his reaction. Anytime someone takes a level one conversation and jumps it up to level ten, it's telling. And what it tells you is that there's another conversation happening inside that person's head that you weren't invited to. Something hidden has taken over their filter and is now driving their reactions. You're only seeing the tip of the iceberg.

What else is at play? Who am I really talking to? I intended to find out.

Having let about ten seconds pass from his last words—"lawyers are the worst thing to happen to America"—I gave a soft smile and said slowly, "Well, maybe you're right." I waited another ten seconds as I sat back in my chair and moved my gaze around the room. When I was ready, I leaned forward and put my forearms on the table. "Tell me, please. What's been your biggest struggle this year?" I asked.

Bobby LaPray's eyes looked up to meet mine. "Say what?" he scoffed.

I repeated, "What's been your biggest struggle—personal struggle—this year?"

At that question, Bobby LaPray slowly dropped all emotion from his face. He got very still. I stayed quiet while his eyes seemed to search for the words. After a while, he finally spoke. His words stumbled out, choppy and hesitant, like he was embarrassed to mention it.

"I, uh, I had to put my mother in an assisted living facility last month. My—my dad has long passed, and my brother moves around a lot as a roughneck. So I'm the only one. The only one here to really help her. It's a lot of paperwork and legal stuff I don't understand."

Unlike the Bobby LaPray who had angrily run me up one side and down the other not two minutes ago, this Bobby LaPray was different. When he talked, he looked defeated. He looked scared. And somehow, he looked small.

Letting his words sink in, a few seconds later I responded gently, "I'm sorry. I can't imagine what that's like." He nodded slightly with pressed lips.

"But what I can tell you is"—I made sure to catch his eye—"you're a good son."

Immediately, Bobby LaPray threw his face down to keep me from seeing it. His huge shoulders shook. And like ice melting off a rock, big Bobby LaPray began to cry.

I quickly told the court reporter to go off the record for a break. "It's okay," I reassured him. "I'm just going to sit here with you."

Through tears, Bobby LaPray poured out all his fears over his mother's health. He told me about the intimidating letters threatening to foreclose his mother's house that he'd been receiving from none other than . . . lawyers. He shared how the banks and government were asking him for things he didn't understand. He felt helpless. He wished his father were still alive. My heart broke for him. He was living in a world I knew nothing about. I thought of Evan.

Bobby LaPray had been holding the weight of it all by himself. For twenty minutes, we sat there as he let it all out. With his attorney's permission, I asked for Bobby LaPray's email address. Sitting there, I cc'd him on an email from my phone to a local colleague who handled elder law and estate planning. She replied minutes later, happily agreeing to set up a meeting with Bobby LaPray the next Monday.

"Thank you," he told me.

"Absolutely," I said. "You good?" I asked.

He took a big sniff, wiped his nose with his sleeve, and sat up.

"Yeah," he answered with a weak grin. "I'm ready."

And for the rest of the deposition, I spoke to the real Bobby LaPray. His answers were direct and forthcoming. His words were more lighthearted. He became more animated, even cracked a few jokes. He no longer looked like he was ready to launch me into oblivion.

"All done," I said finally. "That's all the questions I have. Thank you for your time."

As we all stood up, I walked toward the door and stuck out my hand. I braced for another painful death grip. Instead, at the last second, Bobby LaPray opened up his arms and bear-hugged me. All I could do was smile and say, "Be good."

I didn't look, but I'm fairly sure my feet weren't touching the ground.

The Person You See

I've had countless interactions like that one throughout my life. Sometimes the other person is the Bobby LaPray. Other times, I'm the Bobby LaPray. But why does it happen? How is it that by dropping the idea of winning an argument, you get more of what you want? What is it about connecting to the other person that gives you the high ground? And how can you tap into that strength in your own communication?

It's easy to believe that communication should be cut-and-dried. A world where you say, "You're wrong," and the other person immediately replies, "Why yes, yes, I most certainly am." A place where, when someone says, "I'm fine," the only possible interpretation of the phrase is that they're totally and unequivocally fine. Where what you see on the outside is all there is to someone on the inside, and the boot always fits. That's how you think it should be. That's what you want it to be.

But that's not the way it is.

When you tell someone that they're wrong, they become more convinced that they're right. When someone says they're fine, they're often anything but. It's never as simple as matching stereotypes. Given these problems, I want to go ahead and acknowledge a central theme of this book, and I hope you let this coin drop from your head to your heart:

The person you see isn't the person you're talking to.

Think of a river and its undercurrent. On the surface, your eyes and ears can pick up a person's physical cues that shape your perception and judgments about them. But what's happening below the surface is where their real truth runs. For instance:

- The coworker you **see** is agitated and impatient. The coworker you're **talking to** didn't sleep well last night because he's worried about convincing his brother to go to rehab.

- The cashier you **see** is scattered and inattentive. The cashier you're **talking to** is worried about affording her kids' back-to-school supplies.

- The spouse you **see** is tense and short-fused. The spouse you're **talking to** had a horrible day at work starting with an email from a rude client.

Or, in my case, the mountain of a man I saw was aggressive and defensive. The Bobby LaPray I was talking to, on the other hand, felt alone and worried about his mother. It's this other person you're talking to—the person you don't know—who you need to reach for when conflict starts to tear you apart. Understanding that there's more beneath the surface is one thing, but figuring out how to connect with their deeper self is another. How exactly are you supposed to reach them?

The Struggle You Hear

When Bobby called my questions stupid, everything inside me wanted to prove him wrong. In that instant, the needs of the case took a back seat to **my** needs. My desire to be seen as right blinded me to any other options. I wanted to win. It's what I'm expected to do.

"Oh, you're an attorney? You must win a lot of arguments." I hear it all the time. It's also not true.

Thanks to the countless books out there claiming to teach you how to win every argument, that's all anyone thinks you're supposed to do. **Win.** So let me tell you now. If that's why you're reading this book, go ahead and return it. The sales pitch of winning an argument is overused and overpromised. That's not this book, and I'll tell you why.

For one, you can win an argument and still be wrong.

And second, even if you win, you still come up empty-handed.

Winning an argument is a losing game. Winning means that you've likely lost something far more valuable—their trust, their respect, or worse, the connection. The only reward you've won is their contempt.

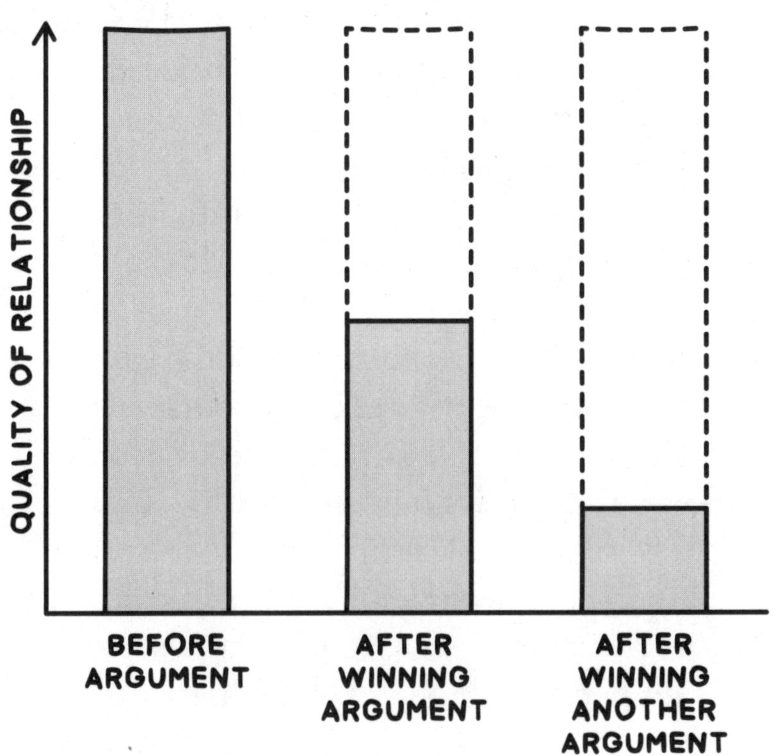

And for what? The argument ends. The conversation is over. You won, congratulations. Now what do you got? The same unresolved issue at the cost of hurt feelings and awkward silence. Most likely, you still have to find a way to communicate with this person. You still have to live with them, to work with them. Depending on what you said, you may now be the one who owes an apology. Any feeling of pride is short-lived compared to the lasting damage to the relationship.

Trial attorneys don't even win arguments. They don't get to choose their clients' facts. They don't get to choose which law to follow. Everything has to pass through a filter of admissibility, then it's up to the judge or jury to apply the law to the evidence. It's more about giving the facts a voice than it is about winning an argument.

Competition in communication has convinced society that the world is divided into "right" and "wrong," "winners" and "losers." After a political debate, the first question someone asks the next morning is always, "Who won?" But if we go back in time to the ancient Greeks, discourse had nothing to do with winning. A debate over opposing issues was a vehicle for pursuing truth. Exposing the weakness in another's argument was to strengthen and refine it, not dismiss it. Debates were known to last for days, even weeks, to give each person time to obtain perspective and explore divisive issues.

Today, the tendency is to do just the opposite.

Rather than allowing disagreement to open you up to learning from another's perspective, you shut it down. Instead of refining your own understanding, you treat it as a threat. We run to social media like it's our own personal megaphone to voice just how much we disagree.

Be honest. How many times has a social media post disparaging your point of view ever changed your mind? And how many times has something you posted that criticized someone else's opinion ever changed theirs? Never. The world turns, the news cycle moves on, and the next day, no one cares. So, what then? What did you prove?

The fastest way to lose your peace of mind is to give someone a piece of yours. Beating out someone in an argument may feed your ego, but it'll still leave you hungry. Rarely, if ever, does winning in communication lead to better things in your life. That's why I care enough about you to tell you the truth:

Never win an argument.

Whether it's an argument, a heated discussion, or slight friction in conversation, your goal isn't to "win." It's to **unravel**. Start at the loose ends until you understand the heart of the matter. There you'll find the knot.

This is a book of knots. The hard stuff in social relationships that, admit it, you'd rather skip over. Untying crossed wires takes time, takes emotion, takes effort. That's what conflict in communication represents: a struggle.

An argument is a window into another person's struggle. In every difficult conversation, there's a moment when someone—whether it's you or the other person—hits a snag. Maybe you don't understand what they're trying to say. Maybe you're in a bad mood. Maybe you disagree. It's not the clash of opinions; it's the clash of worlds, of the very way you see things. Behind every harsh and uncut word, there's a backstory, a why. And if you can find the discipline to get to that, if you can peel back the layers of the argument to discern the struggle, the fear, or the hope hiding underneath, that's where real communication begins.

Because at the end of the day, it's not about the argument. It's about seeing through the keyhole into another person's world and realizing that maybe, just maybe, the win you thought you wanted isn't what you needed after all.

The Challenge to Accept

Most people understand that success comes from seeing failure not as a setback, but as a stepping stone. Embracing failure is part of the process. You learn from your mistakes to grow stronger. Failures to communicate, as in disagreements and arguments, do the same thing. They lead to success because they reveal areas of improvement, offering insights into how you can enrich your interactions. The bigger the conversation, the bigger the need to handle conflict effectively. When done right, conflict isn't a fight. It's an opportunity. It's a catalyst for real, meaningful connection, if you're willing to see it.

What life experiences have shaped how you see conflict?

When you were a kid, defiantly shouting "No!" or bombarding adults with "Why?" was your way of figuring things out. Cause and effect. As a teenager, those simple childhood reactions turned into more complicated questions about finding your place and your identity apart from your family. The clothes you wore, the music you listened to, even the clique you hung around, were statements of who you wanted to be. Stepping into adulthood, disagreements became less about asserting individuality and more about coexisting with other people. Your conversations turned to topics like children, career paths, and mortgages. Or in my case, what vacuum to buy and whether that piece of furniture I found in my parents' garage still had "good bones." As an adult, the stakes change. Your responsibilities grow as you have to think collectively, now responsible for people other than yourself, such as aging parents or your own children. You take interest in broader issues like politics, news, and global affairs.

Despite your age, things may feel even more uncertain. When that happens, you tend to fall back to what you know—your lived experiences and the behaviors modeled for you growing up.

Ask yourself: How did watching arguments in my childhood influence the way I argue now?

If yelling and aggression were the go-to methods for conflict in your home growing up, you might find yourself thinking that's just how things are done, even if you know it's not the best way to get your point across. On the flip side, if you came from a place where everyone tiptoed around disagreements to save face or avoided conversations out of fear of what the neighbors might think, diving headfirst into arguments might make you feel uncomfortable.

Take this one time I stayed over at a friend's house during the summer as a kid. His parents got into a massive shouting match right in front of us—doors slamming, the works. I remember being absolutely mortified. I grew up with parents who kept their arguments private, either hashing things out in their room or waiting until we were asleep. So, seeing his parents go at it, I was positive that a divorce was unfolding before my eyes. But my friend? He didn't even blink. To him, it was just a typical Tuesday night.

Looking back, maybe you're not thrilled with how conflict was handled around you. Maybe you have bad memories of seeing arguments bring out the worst in the people you loved. Maybe you've caught yourself echoing their words or mirroring their actions—even in the little things, like how you move your hands or the tone of your voice. You've gotten to a point in your life where you're beginning to realize that what you observed wasn't that healthy. And you can't help but wonder, would things have gone easier for you in your own life if you'd seen better ways to deal with conflict?

If that's you, then I'm asking you to take on the challenge and break the cycle.

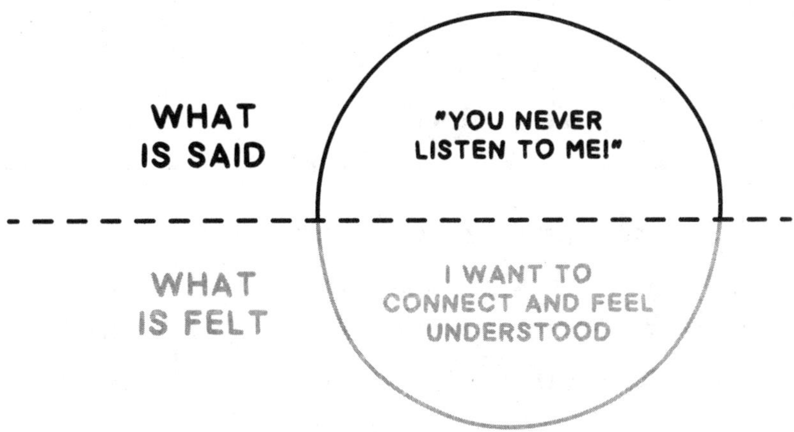
WHAT
IS SAID
"YOU NEVER
LISTEN TO ME!"
WHAT
IS FELT
I WANT TO
CONNECT AND FEEL
UNDERSTOOD

Stop seeing arguments as something to win but as an opportunity to understand the person behind the words. Stop hearing only what's said and start hearing what's felt.

Build the discipline to connect to the person in front of you.

Embrace the failures to communicate and learn from them. Reach success by using each misstep as a stepping-stone, and make room for more positive and **real** in your life—like a bear hug from a man who until recently wanted to shot-put you.

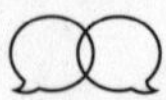

Now, it's highly likely that the themes in the pages ahead won't be anything new to you. You know you should speak with confidence and control your emotions. You know you should avoid getting defensive and stand up for yourself. The question you have is "Yes, **but what does that look like**?"

Well, it starts with what you say next.

CHAPTER SUMMARY

- The person you see isn't the person you're talking to. Every person has a surface and a depth. Often, the emotions you hear in someone's voice are not bids for disagreement but bids for connection.

- Don't buy into the lie that you need to win an argument. When you seek to win, you tend to lose much more, like the other person's trust or respect. Instead, view arguments as a window into another person's struggle.

- Conflict can be a catalyst for positive changes in your life. To harness it, you have to be willing to connect with the person opposite you.

- Turning your conflicts into connections paves the way for a more fulfilling, meaningful life. All you need is in what you say next.

CHAPTER 2

Your Next Conversation

Bzzz.

You look down at your phone to see a text you weren't expecting: "I'm ready to talk."

It's a friend—at least, you're pretty sure it's a friend. A few weeks ago, the two of you had a fight that ended with you calling them selfish and attention-seeking. They called you dismissive and controlling. Neither of you wanted to give in and reach out to the other. But you have so many friends together that it's impossible not to run into each other. You're still not speaking. Honestly, it's gotten pretty awkward.

Rereading the text, you almost feel like you won the holdout, but you were ready to talk last week. Now you're ready to put your pride aside. "Me too," you respond. "Lunch tomorrow?"

A few seconds later your friend replies, "Sounds good. Talk soon."

Fast-forward to the two of you sitting across from

each other at lunch. After small talk, you break the ice. "What you said really hurt me."

"I hurt **you**?" your friend says in an accusing tone.

You repeat yourself. "Yes, what you said hurt me. You didn't even care."

Your friend nearly cuts you off. "Well, I wouldn't have said it if you hadn't reacted the way that you did."

Wait, you think to yourself, **that's not what's supposed to happen. That's not what they were supposed to say.** In your mind, you had pictured your friend apologizing and realizing how terrible they'd been. Slowly shaking your head, your nostrils flare and your eyebrows point down. **You want to go there? Fine.**

You fire back, "Me? No. You started this."

Your friend quickly responds, "I just find it funny how you . . ."

And there it goes.

The conversation sinks right back down to where it was weeks before. You tell yourself, **This was such a mistake. I'm so stupid for thinking that they'd do anything other than think about themself.** Yet you still argue. You know you should probably surrender some ground to try to salvage the conversation, but no. Now it's the principle of it. **I'm right**, you remind yourself. All the while, your friend is thinking and feeling the same thing. After a few more minutes of back-and-forth, your friend says, "You know what? Forget it. I knew this was going to be a waste of time," and abruptly leaves.

You're left sitting with the check and a half-eaten lunch with no desire to finish it. You wonder if the friendship is over for good. You wonder if you even care. But as soon as you have that thought, you realize you **do** care and you're not ready to give up.

You wish you'd had the right words the first time.

The Power of Your Next Conversation

The only thing guaranteed in communication is that you're bound to say the wrong thing. The good news is that it doesn't have to stay wrong. That's why your next conversation often matters more than your first.

You can change **everything** in your next conversation.

Yes, initial conversations, like meeting someone for the first time and making that first impression, are important. But it's the **next** conversation that tests whether your first impression will remain a lasting one. That job interview, that first date, that initial meeting, everyone has their guard up. Everyone is on their best behavior. Over time, the shine wears off, and the person you thought you knew may turn out to be someone completely different. That exciting new hire turned out to be a terrible team player. That person you liked enough for a second date said something that has ensured there won't be a third. And that project meeting where everyone said they liked your plan? Turns out no one was really crazy about it. There's something about these follow-up conversations that makes people feel more comfortable voicing what they tiptoed around initially. In this way, next conversations can be closer to the truth.

They're also more healing. Take a heated argument, for example. Tensions mount and the two of you may begin shouting. After you've exhausted enough energy, the momentum of the conversation slows to a halt. It may be minutes. It may even be years. But eventually you find your way back to each other for the next conversation. The second time around, you tend to speak with lower voices and fewer reactions, or say things like "What I meant to say was . . ." You both want to mend and restore. The next conversation has the benefit of hindsight and reflection, an understanding of what was missing from the first go-around. There's so much you can do in the next conversation: reframe, apologize, laugh over it.

You know this.

One reason you may be reading this book is because you've already had plenty of conversations—too many conversations—with that difficult person in your life. You're here because you need to know how to handle the next one. Who will your next conversation be with? What conversation needs to happen but hasn't yet? Throughout this book, envision applying these methods to the various opportunities for communication in your life.

Everything you want to say, and how you want to say it, can be found in the next conversation.

Why Your Conversations Need Goals

There is, however, one major caution with next conversations: don't rely on the way they play out in your head.

You can rehearse that difficult talk with your friend a dozen times and still come up short. Why is that? Why do conversations go so perfectly in your mind, only to crash and burn in real life?

The answer is because your goal set you up for disappointment.

When you choose goals for conversations that are unrealistic or unmanageable, you're expecting too much from the other person, including yourself. I know it sounds weird to say this, but you're setting the bar too high. You're swinging for the fences when all you need is a base hit.

Instead of telling yourself, "I must fix everything right now," or "Everything must go back to exactly how it was before," make your goal more reachable. It can be as simple as "I want to hear their perspective without getting defensive," or "I want to listen without interrupting." Rather than demanding the moon, take that one small step toward understanding each other better.

At the most basic level, your goals for every conversation should align with this mindset:

Have something to learn, not something to prove.

When you set your sights on smaller, more attainable objectives focused on learning rather than proving, you're more likely to have productive conversations that point you in the direction of success.

WHEN YOUR CONVERSATION HAS GOALS

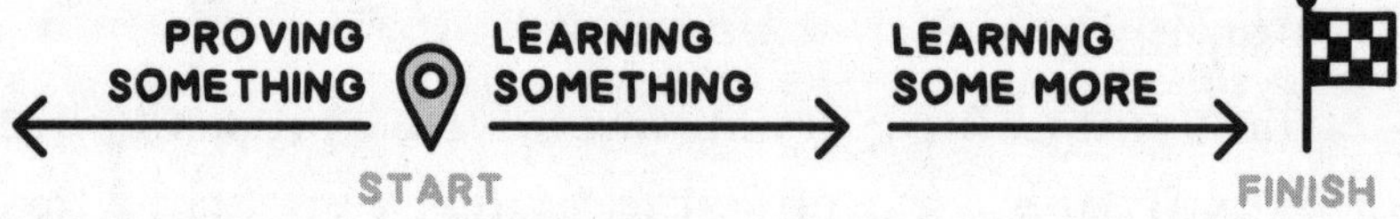

Back in the friend lunch example, you had no real idea of what you wanted out of the meeting before you sat down at the table. That is, aside from your friend confessing that you were 100 percent right and they were 100 percent wrong. Only after they started groveling would you, as the merciful friend you are, accept them back into your good graces.

Yeah, that's never going to happen.

Entering a difficult conversation without a plan and simply hoping for a perfect outcome solely in your favor is a sure way to end up disappointed. Intentionally approaching a difficult conversation with clear, realistic goals is how to create real change. Emphasis on **realistic**.

Compare these pie-in-the-sky goals with those that are actually within reach:

- Unrealistic goals:
  - Hoping for an immediate apology and an admission of "You were right"
  - Expecting them to accept your opinion without question
  - Believing one conversation will cure all other underlying relationship problems
  - Assuming the discussion will naturally lead them to seeing everything from your perspective
  - Thinking they will concede and fall on the sword of every point you throw out

- Realistic goals:
  - Ensuring that the other person knows you care about them
  - Gaining a better understanding of where the other person is coming from
  - Agreeing on steps to mitigate or eliminate recurrence of the issue
  - Acknowledging each other's feelings without judgment
  - Leaving the conversation feeling heard, even if agreement isn't reached

See the difference?

You'll get blind acceptance of your point of view zero out of ten times, but you can absolutely get a better understanding of the other person's point of view nine times out of ten. By setting realistic goals, you're framing the conversation around expectations you can meet. To find the goal for your next conservation, try asking yourself questions like these:

1. If I had to choose, what's the one thing that I'd need them to understand?
2. What small step can I take to show them that I heard them?
3. What assumptions am I making?
4. How can I show gratitude for this opportunity to talk?
5. Is there a part of this that I'm trying to win?

Answering these questions will help you formulate goals that will help you get to where you're going in the conversation. Mind you, you're only halfway done. A goal is just a destination. You also need a means of getting there.

Why Your Conversations Need Values

Values in conversations serve as your compass, ensuring that your goals set the direction of what you truly find important, fulfilling, and meaningful. No matter the terrain of the subject up for discussion, your values always point you to true north. Rather than putting emphasis on the other person, your conversational values answer the question, "How will I show up for myself?" That is, who do you want to be seen as **after** the conversation ends?

Here's a quick example. Let's say your goal for the conversation is to leave feeling heard and your value is honesty. At the end of the talk, the other person asks, "We good?" Typically, you'd be tempted to quickly say yes just to get it over with. But deep down, you still don't feel heard. Instead of a flippant agreement, you respond, "I appreciate what you've shared, and I understand where you're coming from. I still don't feel like I've been fully heard on my end." By staying true to your value of honesty, you've ensured that you will reach your goal while also staying true to yourself.

Values project an image of who you are and what you stand for. In conversations, they also inform the behaviors that influence how you listen, respond, and engage. When you align your conversation with your values, you're prepared to meet your goal **before** the conversation even starts.

Think of times in your life when you most felt like yourself. It doesn't mean it has to be your happiest memory. Maybe it was when you were helping someone, or when you stood up for something. Reflect on what values you expressed. Was it compassion? Justice? Fairness? Think on the values you find important in your closest friends.

An easy exercise to help you find your personal values is to poll the person who knows you best, like a close friend, your partner, or a family member. Ask this person each of the following questions and write down their response.

1. What do you think I find important in my life based on my daily conversations?
2. What are three words you would use to describe my character to someone who doesn't know me?
3. What topics of conversation do I get most enthusiastic about?
4. What quality is most important to me in the friendships I have?
5. What emotion do you wish I'd show more of?

There isn't a right or wrong answer, though the responses might surprise you. The poll is simply to help bring into focus the image you currently put out into the world. With their feedback, take some time to yourself. Reflect on topics of your legacy—who you want to be, what you want to be known for, and what good you want to put out into the world. It might take a few hours. It might take a few weeks, or even a month or two, to internalize and identify your personal values. That's okay. It's worth the time spent. And keep in mind, the values don't have to be a single word. They can also be phrases or full sentences. Whatever makes sense to you in your head. In the spirit of fairness, here are mine:

- Where there is room for kindness, I will use it.
- Tell them who I am without saying my name.
- If I can't be a bridge, I'll be a lighthouse.

My personal values highlight the things important to my own personality. For one, kindness makes me think of my momma, and the way she treats everyone. And more so, I want to treat others with kindness regardless of their behavior. I want my actions to speak louder than my words. And I want to be a steady source of light, a safe place they can come back to, even when resolution isn't immediately possible. These values help align me behind every communication that I have. Internal struggles over what to say or how to behave in times of conflict resolve themselves when I respond with my values.

And that's the point. You don't have to agonize over what to say or how to say it. You don't have to second-guess whether the other person deserves their own medicine. Your values make the tough decisions for you. When you align your communication with your values, you increase the likelihood of reaching your goal and ensuring that when times get tough, the real you shows up. But that means the hard work has to happen **before** you open your mouth.

Got it? Good. Now let's rewind the tape.

Bzzz.

You look down at your phone to see a text you weren't expecting: "I'm ready to talk."

After arranging tomorrow's lunch meeting with your friend, you decide on your approach. Instead of passively expecting that the conversation will magically go in your favor, or that your friend will suddenly see the light, you spend time thinking about a proactive approach. You set a goal of gaining a better understanding of each other's perspectives. You choose gratitude as your guiding value, a feeling of thankfulness for this friend and the memories you've shared. And now you're ready for a redo.

As the two of you sit down, you say, "Thank you for meeting with me."

"Yeah, of course. I wanted to," your friend replies.

You lead the conversation. "I could've done better."

Your friend replies, "Me too."

A little more at ease, and with your goal and values still in mind, you take a breath and continue. "Help me better understand what you were trying to tell me. What did I miss?"

And for twenty minutes, your friend pours out their insecurities over things you had no idea about.

Things that, had you taken the opportunity to learn, wouldn't have led you both to where you are now.

You don't interrupt. You don't rebut or justify. You only listen.

Having felt heard and acknowledged, your friend relaxes.

"Can I share what I saw from my perspective?" you ask.

"Yes, I think that would help me," your friend says.

Soon, it's all water under the bridge as you two continue to share your feelings and perspectives.

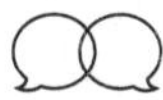

When it's time for you to walk into your own next conversation, don't just rely on how it went in your head. Be realistic. Be intentional. These questions will help:

1. What is my goal for this conversation?
2. Which of my values do I need to meet that goal?

By keeping conversational goals and values in mind, you put connection within reach. Who will your next conversation be with? What conversation needs to happen but hasn't yet? Rather than trying to solve all your problems in one fell swoop, focus on one smaller, more manageable conversation. Then later, have another. And another, until connection is made. Take advantage of the power of your next conversation.

The foundation of every strong relationship is built on this mindset, where the aim isn't to win but to connect, share, and grow together, day after day, year after year. Let your next conversation be an opportunity to practice this clarity in goals and values.

CHAPTER SUMMARY

- Your first step toward connection is as easy as your next conversation.
- Believing that a difficult conversation will go exactly as you heard it playing out in your mind is setting yourself up for disappointment.
- Stop putting too much pressure on a single conversation. Lower your expectations and build on the mindset of having something to learn, not something to prove.
- Set realistic targets for the conversation aimed at gaining understanding instead of grabbing for quick (and unrealistic) wins. Support the goal with your values, the rules you'll follow to make sure you show up as your authentic self.

CHAPTER 3

The Truth About Connection

A while back, my momma randomly texted me. She asked me about the family's white Nissan, the car I'd driven during law school that had been passed down through my siblings. It sat in the driveway of my parents' house. I hadn't driven it in years. This is the verbatim text exchange:

MOM: Do you know how many miles are on the white Nissan?

ME: No ma'am.

MOM: You don't have any idea what the mileage is?

ME: No ma'am.

MOM: Ok, I thought you'd know how many miles were on the white Nissan.

ME: Momma, I don't know how else to tell you. I don't know the mileage on the white Nissan.

MOM: That's fine, Jefferson. I just don't like your attitude.

Honestly, it made me laugh. And thankfully, she wasn't standing in front of me. I called her almost immediately to do what the texts could not—convey my lighthearted tone, provide assurance of my sincerity, and offer a heartfelt apology.

Have you ever had a text conversation suddenly start to turn into an argument when you weren't even upset? Or have you ever misread or misconstrued someone's tone or feelings toward you based on an email or online message? Why is it that despite all this technology to make communication easier, it seems harder than ever?

The answer is that you're not connecting at a level that conveys emotional nuance. You're simply transmitting pixels arranged to display as words and expecting the same result.

You're living in a world of transmission, not connection.

True connection involves sharing information with depth. It gives way for delivery and context. It touches your deepest needs for belonging, understanding, and expression.

Transmission, such as text, email, and the like, focuses on sending and receiving signals through a cold medium. It's transactional. It cares only about processing and conveying data. Transmission is efficient, to be sure, but indifferent to understanding and authenticity.

You see the problems presented by transmission every day. It's the reason people write things in the comment section of social media apps that they'd never say to someone's face. It's why texts and emails can easily be misinterpreted. It's why people feel protected behind a keyboard. With transmission, the human connection isn't there.

Did my mom hear my texts as words in her head? Oh, she read them all right. But she needed my voice to hear my true meaning.

Please don't misunderstand me. There is absolutely a place and a purpose for remote interaction in today's digital landscape. Where you go wrong, however, is when you believe transmission is a replacement for connection. It's not. That's like thinking reading sheet music is going to give you the same feeling as hearing a symphony perform it, or that a description of a sunset will feel the same as seeing it with your own eyes. Transmission conveys information, but connection breathes life into it.

You're meant to feel the warmth of a smile, not read it in an emoji.

What Is Connection?

Here's where I recognize that the word **connection** can be a bit oversold, sort of like telling someone to "be mindful." It sounds good and all, but what does it truly mean?

At a base level, **connection** is a dressed-up word for understanding and acknowledgment. Think of it as a two-factor authentication. You can't have one without the other to connect. If I understand you but you can't tell, you won't connect with me. And if I acknowledge what you're saying but I still don't understand it, I won't connect with you. You need both the internal process of understanding and the external process of acknowledgment to make connection.

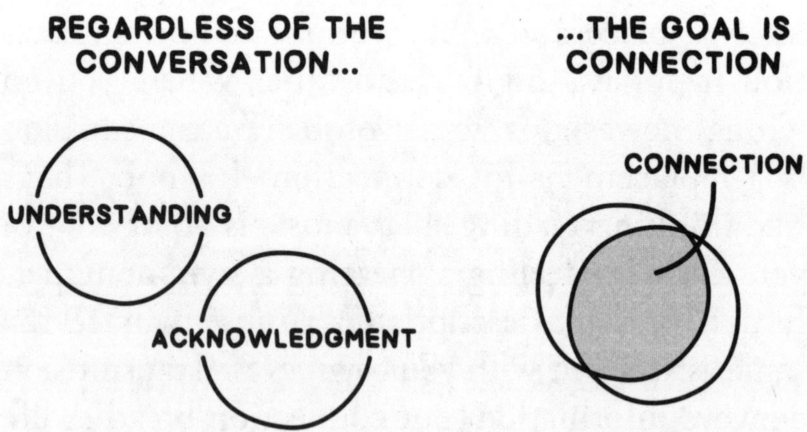
REGARDLESS OF THE CONVERSATION...
...THE GOAL IS CONNECTION
UNDERSTANDING
ACKNOWLEDGMENT
CONNECTION

To me, connection is where you decide to roll up your sleeves and approach the conversation for what it is instead of what you want it to be. I can understand and acknowledge you without agreeing with what you said. I can understand and acknowledge you and still be upset with you, hurt by you, or sad.

I can remember as a teenager being upset about something feeling unfair and voicing my disagreement. My dad would always say, "You don't have to like it. You just need to understand it." Back then, as you'd imagine, I didn't appreciate that very much. But as I grew older, I started to see the wisdom in what he was saying. He was allowing me the space to disagree. He was making sure that he connected with me so I understood why.

People hear "connection" as it relates to conflict and often associate the word with turning negatives into positives, where it's all about happy things and feel-good Hallmark movie moments. That's not the world you or I live in. Connection is both positive and negative. It's a conduit for the happy and the sad, the easy as much as the difficult. It's both. You can't choose the outcome of a conversation. You can only choose whether to try to connect.

And here's another truth: Sometimes not connecting is the right choice. Sometimes disconnection **is** the answer. Not every conversation needs connection. Maybe you've heard about connection in terms of trying to meet someone "on their level" or "where they are." I disagree that it's a hard-and-fast rule.

There are some interactions in which you shouldn't be meeting them anywhere near their level. There are some conversations in which you shouldn't be within a thousand miles of where they are. Some people don't want to be reached. That doesn't make you a failure. That often makes you wise.

So much of what's written about communication nowadays gets caught up in the idea that you're supposed to create easy conversations, in which everyone leaves happy and comfortable. Honest communication has nothing to do with what's happy or comfortable. Connection sometimes means having conversations that are going to be uncomfortable. What you need is the control and the confidence to have them anyway.

Three Ways You Cut Off Connection

In theory, communication should be simple. I say something, you understand it, you say something back, and I understand it. Piece of cake, right? Pfft. Everyday communication is littered with problems: misinterpretation, interruption, defensive behavior, and overreaction. Some people aren't aware of these problems that impact their lives. Others simply lack the skill or practice to get past them without causing more problems. When your communication falls flat, it's usually because one or more of three common things cut the connection.

Cut 1: Lack of awareness

During a heated discussion, have you ever heard someone snark, "Do you even hear yourself right now?" The truthful answer is no, you don't.

No, I mean really. You don't. The sound we hear in our head when we speak actually comes from vibrations through our **bones**. The vocal cords travel up through your skull into your inner ear and make your voice sound deeper and richer. The sound you hear when you listen to a recording comes from sound waves through the air, which make your voice sound thinner or "off" compared to what you'd expect. That's why if you've ever watched a video or listened to a recording of yourself, you may think, "Wait, is that my voice? Is that how I sound?" That's because it's not. Not to you, anyway.

It should be no surprise, then, that you're woefully unaware of what others see, hear, or experience when you talk. Unaware of your volume, your tics, or your verbal fillers. Ever had someone tell you they didn't like your tone when you thought it was perfectly fine? Or tell you that you're yelling when you didn't feel like you were?

All too often, when you're in conversation with another person, your sense of situational awareness puts you in a position of conflict. This lack of awareness can inject tension into your relationships—almost always unintentionally. Imagine that after a stressful phone call in your office, you unknowingly scrunched your eyebrows and looked upset when a coworker gave a simple hello as you two passed each other in the hall. That coworker might now avoid you, or worse, speak negatively about you to other people, all because you were unaware of your own signals.

You've heard it before: "I thought you were mad at me."

The most difficult awareness to achieve is self-awareness. So tell me. Where is the tension in your shoulders right now coming from? Are you taking full breaths? Why is your jaw clenched? Without self-awareness, you stumble around in the dark, unaware of the toes you step on when you speak and fumbling for the keys to your own well-being.

Awareness allows you to identify how you're feeling in the present moment and to understand why you're feeling a certain way. It allows you to take an emotional self-inventory and to act on your findings. When honed, awareness turns into alignment, a continuous feedback loop that tells you whether your current condition is aligned for the current moment. That alignment gives you control.

Cut 2: Lack of understanding

Trouble comes when you insist on viewing the world through the lens of your own telescope. Try as you may, the harder you push to make them see things your way, the more stubbornly they seem to resist. In a classic disagreement, it is almost always the other person who you expect to bend their way of thinking—not yourself. When neither person makes the effort to understand the other, it leads to hurtful comments like these:

"I can't believe you're voting for that person. How could you be so stupid?"

"You just don't understand!"

"I thought I knew you. It's like we're speaking different languages."

It's often not the difference in belief or opinion that's the problem. It's the failure to understand the difference in **perspective**. When you bother yourself enough to want to know why someone holds a particular belief, rather than simply criticizing the belief because it's different from yours, only then will you begin to appreciate their point of view.

In communication, understanding is thankfully a skill that can be learned. It's also an essential skill. Without the ability to appreciate the other's perspective during conflict, it's like a screen door on a submarine—you're not going to get far. When you possess this ability, however, you're empowered to create deep relationships with lasting success. You reach this understanding not by transmission, but through true connection.

Cut 3: Lack of self-assurance

Being direct can be difficult for many people. There's a fear or discomfort that comes with conflict. This fear typically shows up in the form of physically turning your body away, avoiding eye contact, or crossing your arms. There's also the inclination to look away with your words, using phrases that soften or obscure your true feelings. These passive phrases make you approach the conversation more indirectly; for example:

"Hi, sorry to bother you. So, I was thinking, and you can totally tell me if it's not going to work, but . . ."

". . . and that's why I feel like it could work. Does that make sense?"

"This is probably a dumb question, but . . ."

The lack of self-assurance not only tanks your self-esteem but also stifles your personal growth. When even your own thoughts are treated like an inconvenience, you'll find yourself beginning to hide from the very interactions that could bring out the best in you. It also prevents you from asserting yourself to go where you want to go—to chase that dream, to follow that career, to find that love.

Honesty in communication requires confidence—a connection and confidence that asserts your needs and ensures that your voice is heard, your boundaries are respected, and your number one advocate is yourself.

A Quick Note on Confidence

We're going to go in-depth on confidence in chapter seven. But before you keep reading, there's something that I need you to know now. When you see the word **confidence** in these pages, I want you to hold on to a distinction in the back of your mind. The concept of confidence you're likely more familiar with from your past prioritizes perfection. The version of confidence I'm asking you to adopt moving forward prioritizes grace.

Confidence doesn't mean you're not afraid. It means you do it scared.

Confidence doesn't mean you're always right. It means you tell them when you're wrong.

Confidence doesn't mean you avoid mistakes. It means you embrace them.

Every day I run into just how much of a misconception exists about what confidence is. I receive message after message beginning with "**I wish.**" I wish I could say this, I wish I could say that. People often talk of confidence as if it's a trait you're born with, like how tall you are or how much you resemble a parent. They see it as a standard of perfection. In truth, it's far from it. You'll see. The point I'm making now is that if you read the word **confidence** and struggle to identify with it, or find it challenging to conceptualize, you're holding the right book.

CHAPTER SUMMARY

- How you approach your next conversation can be the difference between building connection and breaking it.
- Misinterpretations in texts, messages, and emails highlight the gap between transmission and connection.
- Connection isn't about agreeing on everything or even positive outcomes. It's a two-part process of understanding and acknowledging each other's viewpoints, even when they differ.
- Lack of awareness, understanding, and self-assurance cut off connection to the other person. Part two of this book will show you how to overcome these issues by applying easy, practical methods that build the connection for you.

PART II

The Application

For those who follow my social media content, you know that I'm not a fan of the fluff. I don't give advice that tells you how to communicate from the sidelines, like you need to "actively listen" or "show empathy" or "keep an open mind." I'd rather leave that kind of instruction to the armchair philosophers—it means well, but it doesn't work well. And what is it really asking you to do, anyway? You need something concrete. Something you can use right away.

That's what you'll get in the following pages.

I've created a function that helps build connection in your next conversation **for you**. It works for my own legal clients, and it will work for you too. The function is simple. And to no one's surprise, it has three steps:

1. Say it with control.
2. Say it with confidence.
3. Say it to connect.

What's "it," exactly? Your view. Your needs. Your truth. It turns these essentials of self-expression that make you the unique, one-of-a-kind person that you are into components that naturally pull out your assertive voice. It may even be a voice you haven't heard before, or one you feel as though you once knew. And that's a really awesome thing.

These three inputs follow a cognitive approach to problem-solving called functional thinking. If it sounds familiar, that's because you've likely seen it before, a long, long time ago in math class. Remember algebra? Yeah, me neither. But if you've ever had to "solve for x," then you've engaged in functional thinking. In a nutshell, functional thinking is about observing patterns in how inputs affect an output.

Stay with me here.

Even if you fell asleep in math class, you understand functions. You use them every day. When you put coffee grounds into a coffee maker, you can expect it'll make you coffee. When you press the down button on a thermostat, you can expect the temperature to lower. Your grandmother's family cake recipe? It's a function. The recipe, framed in a set of instructions, turns ingredients (inputs) into a finished cake (output). You don't sit there asking yourself why an egg is being an egg that day—you just know that if you follow the recipe, or the function, you can predict that you'll get your grandmother's cake.

Now, I can't promise you cake. But I can promise you that if you follow the inputs of the function, the output will be a bolder, more assertive you. Simply by using a recipe aimed at better communication, you can expect results that put the control over the next conversation back into your hands.

Rule 1:

Say It with Control

CHAPTER 4

Control Yourself

This isn't based on a true story. But it could be.

Lilly is three. For the past two weeks, she's been fighting bedtime. Either she wants to stay up long after she should be asleep or she gets out of bed multiple times before finally, thankfully, falling asleep.

John is thirty-three and Lilly's dad. John believes in a flexible nightly routine. If Lilly isn't ready for sleep, he thinks it's totally fine if she plays quietly in her room for thirty minutes until she gets sleepy. He likes the idea of Lilly's independence and listening to her own signals when her body is tired.

For the past two weeks, John's been biting his tongue.

You see, Grace—John's wife and Lilly's mom—believes in strict routines. Lilly's bedtime is eight p.m. No exceptions. Grace feels that consistency and structure are the keys to their daughter getting a restful night of sleep and behaving well the next day.

For the past two weeks, Grace has been bottling her anger.

Now it's eight p.m., Lilly's bedtime, and the nightly show begins.

Precious Lilly, blissfully unaware of the time, is playing with her toys in her room. She looks like she just downed two shots of espresso. Everyone knows she's not going to sleep anytime soon. So when Grace gives her **that look**, Lilly preempts her. Eyes wide in that coercive way seemingly built into every child, Lilly whines, "But I'm not tired yet."

John knows this routine is taking a negative toll on all of them, but he also can't help himself. After Grace goes down the hall, he tells Lilly, "OK, you can play just a little bit longer. But after that it's time to go night-night." John walks to the living room, hoping Grace hasn't heard him.

As soon as he enters, Grace says (a little too loudly), "What did I tell you about that? The answer is no. It's bedtime. She's exhausted." She pauses, then hollers back down the hall, "No, Lilly, it's time to put the toys away, honey! It's bedtime."

John replies (a little too loudly), "She's not a robot, Grace. A few minutes won't hurt anything. It's not her fault that you have a control problem."

The Two Phases of Every Argument

Oof.

Let's leave Grace, John, and Lilly for a moment.

I have to imagine that you've felt this, even if you aren't a parent. We've all been John or Grace in similar situations. We've been short with someone. We've said something we almost immediately regret. We win the immediate conversational battle only to lose the relational war in a race to the bottom.

It doesn't have to be that way.

You can learn how to handle yourself—your words, your emotions, and your body, all of which factor into your conversations—so that heated discussions don't explode. But you have to first understand a few facts about communication and how your body works.

Inside every argument, there's an ignition phase and a cooling phase.

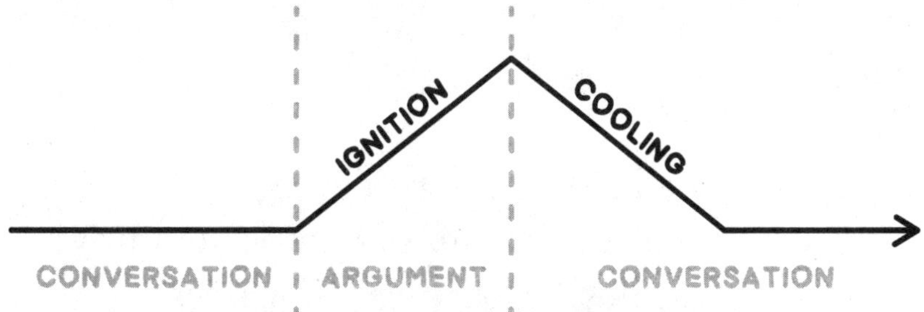

Ignition happens when, with enough friction, the productive becomes destructive. Something about the interaction begins to rub you the wrong way. You resented a word. You didn't appreciate the other person's tone. You didn't like their look. With limited time and enough friction, heat builds. And before you know it, you're on fire.

Ignition happens the moment you:

- Light a match (feel threatened)
- Blow a fuse (get defensive)
- Go nuclear (personal attacks)

When you reach these ignition or heating phases in a conversation, there's a tendency to somewhat forget who you are. Psychologists may refer to this as being "flooded." It's as if you've blacked out the experience entirely. You say things you'd never typically say. You find it difficult to locate your thoughts or decide what you want to say, like a fog over your brain. So you blurt out words, caring little about how they sound, what they'll do, or what they even mean.

Cooling occurs when the heat begins to dissipate. It happens the moment when:

- You turn off the heat (walk away)
- You put out the fire (mutual understanding)
- There's nothing left to burn (impasse)

Whichever route you take, the temperature stops rising and starts to come down. The smoke clears and the frustration lifts. Clarity enters the chat. You regain awareness of the importance of the relationship and why (or if) the other person matters to you.

You know you're cooling when voices lower and tones sound softer. Words are more selectively chosen. Between "I'm sorry I said that" and "I didn't mean it that way," you may exchange apologies or try to clarify meanings. While ignition tends to sound more closed, cooling sounds more open. You may begin to cry. You may begin to regret.

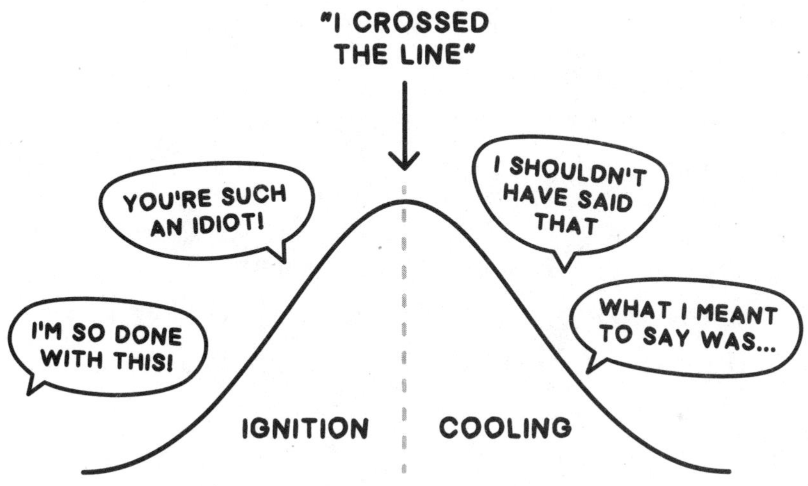

All you know is, you just don't feel great about it.

The hotter the argument burned, the longer it will take to cool down, like turning off the stove and waiting for your cast iron skillet to become cool to the touch. It becomes a matter of degree.

Unfortunately, John and Grace are still far from cooling down.

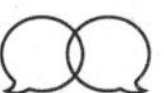

Grace unleashes two weeks of resentment. "This! **This** is why she never listens! Because you **always**

bend the rules! One of us here **actually cares** about her well-being. I'm the one having to deal with her when she's cranky while you get to go do whatever you want! You're **never** here. What would you know?"

If we could pause this exact moment and scan Grace's body, here's what we'd see:

- Her amygdala, the part of the brain that processes emotions, is yelling at her nervous system that a threat is near: she's being undermined.

- Her body has released the hormone epinephrine, or adrenaline, putting her into fight-or-flight mode. She feels it as a prickling sensation and it bristles her tone.

- Her pupils have dilated, allowing more light to enter her eyes so she can focus.

- Her breathing has quickened and shallowed, increasing her oxygen levels.

- Her heart rate is elevated, pumping blood to her body and away from less essential areas, preparing her muscles for action.

- Her shoulders, neck, and jaw go tense.

And most of all, her prefrontal cortex functions are suppressed. That's the area of the brain used for higher-order thinking like rational thought, decision-making, and emotional regulation. With her emotions now taking full control, she throws all caution to the wind. The fight-or-flight response is meant to help us flee or fend off a bear in the wild, not to conduct a discussion about parenting. In this moment, Grace's fight-or-flight mode is unanimously in favor of fight.

To make matters worse, John's body is experiencing the same heating effects.

He yells, "Me?! Oh, what, so now you're saying you're the **only one** who cares about her?" He's in for the fight too, and while losing control, he lights a devastating fuse he hopes will win the battle. "What do you want, for her to end up like your crazy mother? Or worse, like you—lonely and without any real friends?"

Visibly stung, Grace doubles down and goes in for another round. They've both dug in. They continue to fight. Their bodies want to eliminate the threat that the other person represents. As the argument continues, neither Grace nor John truly realizes what they're saying—because the real Grace and John aren't communicating. Their bodies and minds are reacting. Igniting. Doing and saying whatever they can to make the threat go away.

More often than not, ignition phases have to burn

themselves out until, both opponents exhausted, there's a noticeable pause. A brief moment long enough for them to see the damage done. That's when John sees the pain in Grace's eyes. He's crossed the line.

The cooling phase has descended.

If we could pause this exact moment and scan John's body, here's what we'd see:

- He feels drained, both physically and emotionally.
- His nerves die down.
- His focus widens.
- His heart rate and breathing slow down.
- His prefrontal cortex injects his mind with objective analysis.

Reflection gives way to regret.

All John can think is, **Why did I say that? How did I let it get this far?**

Near tears, Grace wonders the same thing. **Why did I blow up like that? Why did I have to say those things? What's wrong with me?**

And just like that, what they started talking about in the first place is forgotten—and Lilly is now fast asleep on her bedroom floor.

How Your Body Controls Your Response

When the heat rises in a conversation, your physiology responds first. Your internal wiring, known as your autonomic nervous system, includes your brain, spinal cord, and all the connections between them and the rest of your body. This nervous system gives you the ability to perceive, sense, feel, emote, behave, and think. It operates below the surface of your consciousness, where involuntary actions are controlled—like how your eyes are moving word-to-word across this page without you having to tell them to, or your mind sounding out each word in your head, all while you're still breathing with a beating heart and hearing the noises around you.

To better control yourself during conflict, you have to know what's happening inside you.

The more technical terms for the ignition phase and cooling phase derive from the two modes of your autonomic nervous system. You are always responding to situations in one of these modes:

- **Fight-or-flight:** This mode is controlled by your sympathetic nervous system.
  - Fight wants to attack: throw a punch, say a hurtful word, stand your ground.
  - Flight wants to escape: leave the room, hang up the phone, ignore the text.

- **Rest-and-digest:** This mode is controlled by your parasympathetic nervous system.
  - Rest wants to recover: step back, pause, take a breather.
  - Digest wants to recharge: store energy, refuel, balance the mood.

As you'd guess, fight-or-flight is your ignition phase. Rest-and-digest is the cooling phase. Normally, when it comes to personal activities or things you do alone, like typing an email or eating a quiet lunch, you don't notice these processes in action. They operate instinctually. But add another person into the mix, where communication is necessary, and the internal signs become much more recognizable, especially in moments of conflict.

So what does this mean for you?

More than you realize, the mere **presence** of conflicting opinions or arguments can activate your fight-or-flight mode. To protect you, your body orchestrates hundreds of unseen changes in seconds that result in a biological response geared toward emotion-driven, rather than logic-driven, behavior. And through that suppression of coherent thinking, your emotions manifest themselves in familiar ways: a defensive comment, a snide comeback, an angry shout, a slammed door, a loud sigh, tears of frustration.

When you get nervous before an important

phone call, hear bad news, or even receive unexpected praise, your brain and body are making micro up-and-down adjustments. These fluctuations in your emotional state are direct responses from your nervous system, which is constantly reacting to perceived or actual threats around you. A rapid heartbeat, shaky hands, flushed cheeks—these are all manifestations of your body's way of processing information and determining how best to make these adjustments within milliseconds.

Equipped with this knowledge, you can look at conversations in a different light. Rather than immediately blaming the other person, you can see your internal response as a natural reaction that requires further digging and curiosity.

Friction offers room for improvement. Because what triggers you teaches you.

Meet Your Triggers

"We need to talk."

When you read or hear that message, what's your first thought?

Let's be honest. **Nobody** likes that message, whether it's in an email, in a text, or face-to-face. Why? It leaves you in the unknown. Your brain tells you there's the potential threat that something is not right, which triggers your ignition mode. The fact that you prepare for the worst is downright biological.

When you experience something you don't like, whether it's heard, seen, or felt, your body can perceive that stimulus as a threat—a trigger. By "trigger" I mean something that causes a strong, negative reaction in you. These triggers can take many forms and are heavily influenced by your personality and childhood, so don't get caught up in thinking your trigger is wrong or inaccurate because it may be different from someone else's.

Broadly speaking, triggers can be categorized as either physical or psychological.

1. Physical triggers

Physical triggers are the most noticeable triggers that hinder communication. They're the easiest to recognize because they involve immediate physical harm, like seeing someone rear back to punch you or an aggressive animal coming toward you. Physical triggers can range from reactions to your environment, such as feeling nervous while hiking close to a cliff edge, to your body's signals, like feeling sick, dehydrated, or exhausted.

Similarly, when you're communicating with others, your body instinctively detects potential dangers to your physical well-being, which can trigger immediate defensive responses. Imagine how the following examples may make you feel physically threatened:

- One of your parents raises their voice or uses a sharp tone while demanding that you obey.

- Your boss steps too close into your personal space during a discussion.

- A coworker angrily points a finger at you during a company meeting.

- Someone unexpectedly grabs your arm to get your attention.

Physical triggers, whether direct or perceived, impact your sense of security and well-being. These triggers provoke protective instincts that override your more logical thinking.

2. Psychological triggers

Psychological triggers are the more frequent type of trigger that hurts our communication. These triggers don't involve direct or expected physical harm. They're simply thoughts, either perceived in the present or anticipated in the future. They arrive in three ways: social evaluation, personal identity, and loss.

Social evaluation triggers

Social evaluation triggers involve the fear of negative judgment, rejection, or humiliation. These perceptual triggers are the questions you ask yourself every day when faced with social interactions:

If I say this . . .
Will they think I'm smart?
Will they get offended?
Will they want to be with me more?

If I do this . . .
Will it be seen as arrogant?
Will I be criticized?
Will they pay more attention to me?

If I look like this . . .
Will I fit in?
Will they make fun of me?
Will they think I'm successful?

Social evaluation triggers can be boiled down to the idea that you care about what others think about you. We all have a deeply rooted need to be liked and desired. You've felt this trigger if you've had to decline an invitation or deliver bad news, or if you've ever experienced FOMO, the fear of missing out. They're all an evaluation of your social contribution: a judgment of how others evaluate your reputation.

The recurring theme in social evaluation scenarios is vulnerability.

Personal identity threats

Whereas social evaluation is concerned with how others perceive you, personal identity is about how you perceive yourself. You recognize these threats as challenges to your competence, autonomy, purpose, or values. They call into question who you believe you are and what you stand for:

1. **Competence triggers:** If I fail, does it mean I'm not capable? If they correct me, am I no longer seen as enough? Example: a professional reenters the workforce late in life only to be met with skeptical remarks from a manager about their ability to keep up the pace, causing them to doubt themself.

2. **Autonomy triggers:** Am I being micromanaged because I'm not trusted? Do I have any say in decisions that affect me? Example: a seasoned nurse or schoolteacher suddenly finds themself micromanaged by a barrage of directives from new administrations, chipping away at their sense of autonomy.

3. **Purpose triggers:** Does my work even matter? Is it making a difference? Am I just going through the motions without any real direction or goal? Example: a once-passionate

Wall Street executive is grappling with a sense of meaning behind their work, no longer comfortable with the crass talk around the office after having a child—their professional identity is now at odds with their new role as a parent.

4. **Value triggers:** Are my beliefs being challenged or disrespected? Am I being pushed to compromise on who I am? Example: a new hire feels his values are under attack when he overhears one of the male senior leaders make a sexually explicit comment about a female intern, creating dissonance between his personal convictions and his workplace.

Each of these scenarios highlights the fact that threats to our personal identity force us to question who we want to be.

You can also feel a challenge to your identity by extension or association. Let's say you hear someone criticize your favorite political candidate. You also feel challenged, even though the criticism is not aimed at you, because you've tied your identity to that candidate or party. Similarly, you can talk bad about your momma if you'd like, but if I talked bad about her, you'd have every right to pop me in the mouth. Why? Because she's helped define your very identity.

Even just hearing the word **no** can be perceived as a personal identity threat. When someone tells you no, doubts you, or says you can't do something, how do you feel? You want to do it even more. You also feel the same way when someone sharply asks you why. Your brain immediately wants to reply, "Because I said so, that's why!" Someone else questioning your choices or actions can be threatening because it calls into question your sense of autonomy.

The recurring theme in personal identity threats is adequacy.

Loss triggers

Loss is the fear of losing someone or something you value, whether it's a person, a job, or a certain status. In communication, you often encounter loss as the fear of losing a relationship or status.

Say you're presenting a proposal at work and a boss raises doubts. Do you push back, defending yourself as the more knowledgeable one? Or do you concede your boss's point and open the floor to further criticism? The immediate fear triggered here is rejection of your proposal, but the underlying fear is the possible loss of your job.

The psychological threat of loss can make you defensive or overcautious in your communication. Perhaps it causes you to overexplain, hesitate to voice your opinions, or avoid difficult conversations altogether. You may often feel this way because the anticipated pain of the loss is stronger than the temporary discomfort of immediate confrontation.

The recurring theme in loss is separation.

Learning about these triggers, you've probably been able to see how they can show themselves in your own life. If you still struggle with knowing what your specific triggers are, just ask a friend. It can be as easy as, "What do you think my triggers are?" If they're a good friend, and if you have a good sense of humor, they'll likely have no problem telling you the truth.

So you've met your triggers. But how do you use this knowledge to improve your communication?

Recognizing your body's ups and downs in the face of conflict gives you a huge advantage. Not only do you better understand your own reactions and triggers, but you'll also begin to identify the signs in the other person.

You could call it emotional intelligence. I prefer to call it discernment, a sixth sense–like ability to pick up on the smaller details. A raising of the voice. An exhale of exasperation. A tensing of the shoulders. They aren't behaviors to get offended over. They're **information to gather**. Data about the emotional state of the person. Instead of getting upset when they raise their voice, you relate to it in your own life as a sign of their body's ignition—it informs you that their body is feeling threatened, either by you or by something hidden from you. Instead of reacting to "win" the argument, which you know now will only trigger more ignition, you respond in a way that triggers cooling. It helps you better gauge the temperature of the conversation. By understanding yourself, you understand the other person.

When you reverse engineer your own triggers, you'll become more skilled at identifying the triggers of others. You'll begin to hear someone's raised voice not as an attack but as a plea to remove the threat. If you want to put out their fire, find their trigger.

CHAPTER SUMMARY

- What triggers you teaches you—if you're willing to learn.
- Inside every argument is an ignition phase and a cooling phase.
- The ignition phase engages the signs of fight-or-flight, like saying something to hurt someone or abruptly leaving the room.
- The cooling phase begins when the temperature of the conflict lowers, like reaching understanding or adding distance between you and the other person.

- There are two main triggers to know: physical and psychological. These triggers arrive through actual or perceived threats to your body that activate ignition. Understanding what triggers are unique to you informs you which areas to work on and which areas to avoid.

- When you reverse engineer your own triggers, you'll become more skilled at identifying the triggers of others. You'll begin to hear someone's raised voice not as an attack but as a plea to remove the threat. If you want to put out their fire, find their trigger.

CHAPTER 5
Control the Moment

Here on the east side of Texas, we have tall pine trees. The woods are so thick with brush that you can't see more than a few yards in front of you. Growing up, my friends and I would make trails, build shelters, and play in creeks, pretending we were in some sort of survival adventure. I have a lot of fond memories in the woods.

One of my favorite things about living around tall trees is when it rains. You can't see the storm rolling in like you can in places where it's flat and open. If you just rely on your eyes, you won't know it's coming until it's already on top of you.

You know it's about to rain because you sense it. Everything slows down. The woods and the animals go quiet. The temperature drops, and the sound of rustling leaves draws closer as a slight wind moves through the trees. You can feel the coolness on your skin. The air electrifies. You smell the rain.

It's in this moment, this calm before the storm,

when the earth hangs in a suspended second of stillness. There's a building anticipation you can almost touch, as if nature is waiting for just the right time to unleash the storm.

Every argument contains the same charged silence. Right before the conflict begins, there's a noticeable change in the emotional climate. Maybe a pause lingers too long, or the tone subtly shifts. A word choice seems out of place.

You know it's about to be a conflict because you sense it.

You can feel yourself, or the other person, about to give way. Like the instant right before a roller coaster takes its first dive.

This is where you're losing out on one of the most crucial moments of control in an argument, and here's why. You're looking for what will control **them**—not what's controlling **you**. You're too busy planning out your opening line. Too occupied preparing to scold or reprimand them. You miss out on the ability to steer the argument because you view the coming storm as only a call to arms, when in reality, this very moment can give you the high ground in every argument.

People miss out on this subtle moment because they're not looking for it. That gives you an invisible advantage before an argument ever begins. You'll never have a better chance for control than when it's quiet, right before the storm hits. So don't waste that chance preparing for them—spend it preparing for you.

In the previous chapter, I told you how your body works in heated arguments. Your next step is to equip yourself with tools that **leverage** what your body already does. Each of these tools requires only a moment to use but offers long-lasting benefits. And the more often you use these tactics, the more leverage you'll have.

To stay in control even in the most chaotic conversations, these are the three most effective tools I've developed:

- Your first word is your breath.
- Your first thought is a quick scan.
- Your first conversation is a small talk.

Like with rain, you often can't stop an argument from coming. But by using these three quick but effective tactics, you'll do more than just weather it. You'll begin to prevent arguments from igniting and control outcomes altogether.

Your First Word Is Your Breath

Not long ago, I presented Elizabeth for her deposition in her personal injury case. The attorney on the other side was notorious for trying to get under people's skin, mine included. Given my run-ins with him in the past, I knew his strategy: hurt Elizabeth's credibility. If he could get her to trip over her words or say something wrong, or if he could force out an emotionally negative outburst, she'd become easier to control—and as a result, he'd have greater influence over the outcome of the case.

Knowing this, I spent hours with Elizabeth preparing for the deposition. To help train her, I changed my tone to mimic the other attorney's. I quickly asked questions, trying to steamroll her for an even faster response.

In a gruff, rushed voice, I asked, "So you had time to see the other car, didn't you?"

Elizabeth gave me a blank stare.

Pretending to be frustrated, I said, "Come on, Mrs. Carson." Then I raised my voice. "It's an easy question. Yes or no. You had the time?"

My pressing caused her to freeze—another symptom of the ignition phase—which resulted in a deer-in-the-headlights situation. She was nervous; her voice shook and her eyes watered, both of which are totally natural bodily reactions. After explaining to her why and how her body was reacting to this aggressive behavior, I introduced a concept that would become her most-used tool.

Your first word is your breath.

I explained it this way: Whenever you're about to begin a sentence, let your **breath** be the first **word** that you say. That is, where your first word might be, put a breath in its place.

Forcing yourself to imagine your breath as a word, as part of the conversation itself, helps you engage the protocols of controlled breathing. These protocols play a critical role in regulating both your body and your emotions. Putting your breath first places you in control from the outset. The first two seconds are the most crucial because they prevent the momentum of your ignition phase from building.

Terms like **breathwork** and **breath control** and **controlled breathing** are all fancy words for putting intention into how you breathe. For example, you've probably breathed just fine reading up to this point. You've given little attention to how much air is moving in and out of your lungs. But if I tell you to breathe in and hold it for five seconds and then release, well, congratulations! You've engaged in breath control, the act of placing attention on the air moving through your body.

Now, take a deep breath in with me and think about your last stressful conversation. Do you recall what your breathing was like? In arguments, your breath typically does one of two things: it speeds up or it locks up. Neither is good.

When your breath speeds up, that's a sign that you've triggered your ignition phase. You have to breathe more to meet the increased oxygen needs of your muscles, which prepare you to run or attack. The faster you breathe, the faster your heart needs to pump blood to keep you oxygenated and alive, increasing your heart rate. When you have rapid breathing, your mechanical abilities to think and speak suffer.

When your breath locks up, you'll feel like you're suffocating or drowning. In some sense, you are. Whereas rapid breathing leads to too much oxygen in your body, little to no breathing leads to too much carbon dioxide because of your failure to exhale. So holding your breath, or shallow breathing, is equally detrimental. As the tension increases, your cognitive ability decreases.

To avoid these problems, your breath needs balance.

Okay, back to Elizabeth.

On the day of the deposition, she started out great. Elizabeth's words were slow and shake-free. But after a while, I could tell that she was beginning to lose confidence. Her voice began to tremble, her responses came out faster, and she was visibly getting annoyed. She was getting defensive. She was losing control.

But that's when the magic happened.

Right before I was going to jump in and ask for a five-minute break, she did it.

Leaning his head forward, the other attorney pressed her. "Fair to say you weren't paying attention at all that day, were you? **Isn't that right?**"

Elizabeth took a breath, lowered her shoulders, and took a half second for herself before calmly stating, "No." Right then, I knew what the opposing attorney didn't: her first word had come **before** the no. It was her breath. And by using the space between his question and her answer to steady herself, she had just taken back control of the conversation.

"What's wrong? Did you not like my question?" the opposing attorney jabbed.

A composed and confident Elizabeth smiled and shook her head. "Oh, no, I like your questions just fine," she said slowly. Hearing this, he tilted his head in confusion. "I appreciate you helping me clarify it," she continued. "Again, the answer is no. That's not fair to say."

Open-mouthed and deflated, the opposing attorney fumbled over his words while trying to find his next question. Seeing that Elizabeth wasn't going to give him the reactions he wanted, he asked a few softball questions and quickly finished.

I was beaming at her.

She couldn't control his questions, so she decided to control herself.

How to Take a Conversational Breath

When your first word is your breath, I call it a **conversational breath**.

I use the word **conversational** because you can do this in the natural flow of a conversation. When done right, it looks just like normal breathing. You can use this technique at any time without looking odd to the other person. But the best time to take a conversational breath is either while the other person is talking and you're listening or shortly before you respond.

Here's how to take a conversational breath:

1. Breathe in slowly through your nose for two seconds.

2. At the top of the inhale, take another quick inhale through the nose for one second. The inhale count is now three.

3. Breathe out through your nose for six seconds, making sure that your exhale is twice as long as your inhale.

4. Repeat the exercise at least twice, or as needed throughout the dialogue.

A conversational breath takes advantage of several different benefits, all backed by scientific studies and the methods of those who've mastered breathing in the most stressful of situations. A conversational breath also incorporates the three following proven factors. The result is a slow, controlled breath that you can repeat in a pattern to keep yourself calm and focused.

When your first word is your breath, breathe like this:

1. To slow down your breathing, breathe through your nose

When you breathe through your mouth, the air doesn't meet resistance. Consequently, you inhale and exhale more per minute. So you breathe faster. And breathing faster, as you know, is a signal of the ignition phase. If gone unchecked, mouth breathing can leave you in a state of low-grade anxiety and stress.

Breathing through your nose, on the other hand, causes greater air resistance. Do me a favor: Try this test. Take a big breath and exhale through your mouth normally. Now take another breath and exhale with your lips barely touching, like you're going to whistle. Finished? On this second breath, the air came out much slower because your opening was smaller. Your nasal passages are of course much narrower than your mouth, so your nose naturally encourages slower, deeper breathing. The very structure of your nasal passages is meant to filter, warm, and humidify the air you inhale.

Nasal breathing also pulls airflow deeper into your lungs using your diaphragm. That keeps your breath fuller. And when you take fuller breaths, you take fewer breaths per minute, preventing signs of ignition.

Now that you're filled with oxygen, let's push the air out, but with purpose.

2. To maintain calm, exhale longer

A 2023 study from Stanford Medicine confirmed powerful benefits associated with a breathing technique known as a physiological sigh, noted as one of the fastest ways to de-stress in real time. The technique involves injecting a controlled, intentional **sigh** into your normal breathing. In doing so, start with a double inhalation, which involves taking a normal breath in through your nose, followed by a second, sharp inhale, and ending with a long exhale through the mouth.

The exhalation should last around twice as long as the inhalation. A double inhale fully inflates the lungs, and a long exhale mimics the effect of the "ah" sound you might release after a big sigh. This method of prolonged exhalation helps lower blood pressure and reduce stress levels in the body. The longer exhalation also makes sure that what you breathe in next is all oxygen and that carbon dioxide gets properly regulated.

When compared with two other breathing techniques, physiological sighing showed the greatest decrease in anxiety, the most improvement in mood, and the lowest respiratory rates. To take advantage of these benefits for yourself, you need to make sure that your exhale is longer, preferably twice as long as your inhale.

Now that you've taken a full breath, you should feel calmer and more in control of yourself. But there's one more crucial step so that your next word after your breath is controlled.

3. To clear your mind, breathe rhythmically

If you don't think your breath has much to do with controlling **verbal** conflict, then it's worth looking at what it means to those who've mastered it at the furthest extremes of **physical** conflict. The Navy SEALs consider rhythmic breathing so mission-critical that they receive special training in what they call "tactical breathing." In combat situations, the influx of adrenaline raises a person's heart rate. This shift causes changes within the body that rapidly deteriorate motor skills, skills that can mean the difference between life and death.

To control this response, the soldiers often use rhythmic breathing, a method that relies on a consistent pattern of a set count between inhalations and exhalations. Box breathing, for example, in which you inhale, hold, exhale, and hold, each for a measure of four seconds, is a pattern of rhythmic breathing. It creates intentionality and regularity in the breath.

The benefit of rhythmic breathing is a lower heart rate, which can sharpen a soldier's mental focus. Rhythmic breathing is one reason you'll hear military personnel yelling out cadence lyrics while they run to **one, two, three, four.** The counting synchronizes their footsteps and, more important, their breath. The repeated pattern not only helps force carbon dioxide out of their lungs, but the steady rhythm also prevents hyperventilation or irregular breathing.

Military personnel, law enforcement, first responders, boxers, fighter pilots, and martial artists regularly face high-stress conflict in which breathwork is essential for both effective performance and survival. If controlling their breath is important enough for them, it's important enough for you.

By taking a conversational breath, you'll leverage the positive effects of intentional breathing. This breath sets the stage for your next action, one that will give you increased control over your body and your responses.

Your First Thought Is a Quick Scan

The room was dark and moody. It smelled like my momma's essential oil diffuser. Once my law school classmates and I quieted down, the yoga instructor told us that we'd be starting with a brief meditation. My eyebrows shot up. I thought, **Like,** meditation **meditation? As in, where you hum and stuff?** Not only had I never tried yoga before, but I had also never meditated. It's not really all the rage in small-town Texas.

Sitting on our mats, we began by closing our eyes

and focusing on taking full breaths. That sounded easy enough. I could do that. After a few minutes of breathing, we then performed what the instructor called a "body scan." With eyes closed, we were told to mentally scan our body, slowly, starting at our feet and moving upward until we reached the top of our head.

I tried to do what the instructor was telling us and the only thing I felt was silly. Maybe I was doing it wrong?

I opened one eye to glance around the room. It seemed to be going fine for everyone else. At that moment I heard the instructor explain that we had to be still enough to listen to our bodies. I honestly wasn't even sure I understood what that meant. I closed both eyes again. Trying to refocus, I took another breath and began to quiet my mind, searching for something.

I waited.

And slowly, much to my surprise, as I scanned upward I noticed physical sensations inside my body that I hadn't picked up on before. Tension in my face and behind my ears. Lifted shoulders. A clenched jaw. Breath that was shallow and uneven. How had I not caught any of this before?

My body had been holding this stress and I didn't even know it.

I quickly adjusted by relaxing the muscles of my face and shoulders. I expanded my breath to use the full capacity of my lungs. I overheard the instructor tell us to label the first emotion that came to mind. The word **pressure** rose to the top.

Instantly, I felt relief. But it was more than that. I felt in control. Even with exams coming up, I immediately felt more at ease and less anxious.

After the class was over and I proved how horrendously inflexible I was, the idea of the body scan stuck with me. The more I went to yoga, the better I got at body scanning. I was fascinated with the ways my stress was hiding. It became something of a game, with me feeling better each time than I had before I'd scanned.

Then I got faster. I could briefly close my eyes at the top of an inhalation, perform a full body scan, then open my eyes on an exhalation. Because my body was getting faster at telling me where the stress points were hiding, I got quicker at locating them and dealing with them. Labeling my emotions also became easier. What was once a five-minute exercise at the yoga studio became a quick two-second reset.

I began to think of what I was doing as a "quick scan," and I started trying it out in different environments, like while in my seat during class and exams: **worried**. While I was at a red light: **impatient**. Studying at the kitchen table at our duplex: **overwhelmed**. Whenever a tense moment bubbled up, a quick scan would dissolve it.

Soon, I learned that if I could do a quick scan before or during a difficult conversation, not only would the conversation go better, but the other person wouldn't even notice. I found that I had increased control over my responses. The ability to hone and attune myself to the sensations and messages of my own body was a game changer in my communication. Anytime my body sensed a trigger during an argument or conflict, I trained myself to release it with a quick scan in order to maintain my composure.

It was like being underwater with a never-ending supply of oxygen—I never felt the need to come up for air. What's more, my quick scans enabled me to better realign my mind to the goal and values I needed for the particular conversation.

How to do a quick scan

This is another four-step process. But the more you practice it, the sooner you'll forget there are any steps at all—it'll become second nature.

1. **Breathe:** Begin with a conversational breath. As you inhale, focus on letting your breath expand into your stomach, as if a string is attached to your belly button and being pulled outward.

2. **Close your eyes:** At the top of the inhalation, when your lungs are full, close your eyes for one to two seconds. It should look almost like a long blink.

3. **Examine:** As you exhale, feel for the places in your body where your stress is hiding. Where do you feel discomfort or tightness? Channel your long exhalation into that part of your body and release the tension. Your eyes should be open.

4. **Label the emotion:** Say in your head what you're feeling in that precise moment. Give it a name. If you can, use just one word. There's no right or wrong answer, this should be instinctive.

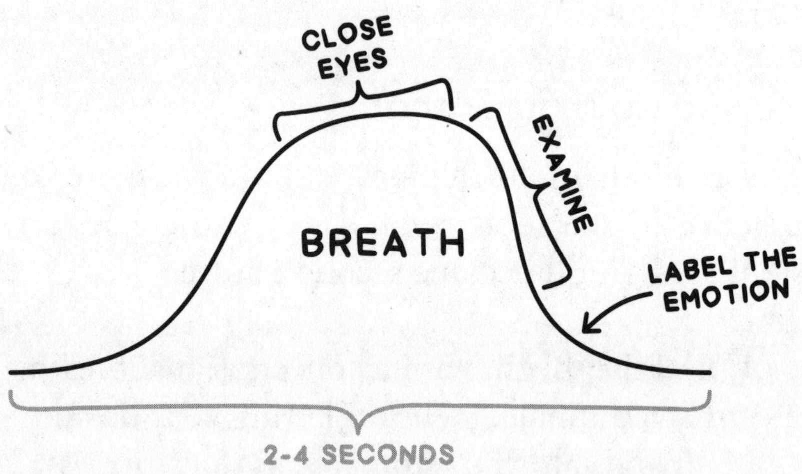

The point of a quick scan is twofold:

- Because it's combined with a conversational breath, quick scanning improves your ability to think clearly in the moment.

- Quick scanning also keeps the control over your emotions in your hands.

Once you get comfortable with quick scans, doing them becomes like taking sips of water during a workout to stay hydrated. You stay focused and fresh. It's a micro-practice of mindfulness that helps you to center yourself and become more self-aware. Gaining greater body awareness also promotes emotional regulation because it enables you to observe your feelings without getting overwhelmed by them.

As you get more comfortable, you can start to incorporate quick scans into real conversations. The phrase "I can tell" is the key to translating your labeled emotion in step four into a verbal communication. You can reframe an internal label like "I am angry" into "I can tell that I'm experiencing the feeling of anger." Instead of keeping your emotions inside and bottling up the stress (which leads to ignition), saying "I can tell" forces you to get those feelings out. For example, sticking with the feeling of anger, you could say out loud, "I can tell I'm getting upset." Your phrasing could also sound like this:

- Unhappy: "I can tell I'm not in the best mood. Can we please talk about this later?"

- Threatened: "I can tell I'm feeling pressured right now. I need time to feel more secure."

- Frustrated: "I can tell I'm getting frustrated. I need a time-out."
- Anxious: "I can tell I'm not emotionally prepared for this conversation right now."
- Unsettled: "I appreciate this conversation. I can tell there's more for me to process."
- Overwhelmed: "I can tell I'm overwhelmed at the moment. Can we take this step-by-step?"
- Confused: "I can tell I'm still confused about what you're saying. Could you tell it to me differently?"
- Nervous: "I can tell I'm a bit nervous about this decision. I need to go over the details again."
- Sad: "I can tell I'm feeling a little overcast. I need some time to myself right now."
- Tired: "I can tell I'm not at my best right now. I need to revisit this after a break."

By verbally acknowledging what you've found in your quick scan, you take out the mystery of what's happening to you and where your compass is pointing—again, keeping you more aware. You've also injected transparency and honesty into the conversation by being open and direct as well as making your needs explicit.

Quick scans are the best way to grab hold of yourself and flip through your layers. The add-on of verbalizing your scan transforms insecurity into a product of confidence and strength.

Because when you claim it, you control it.

In the span of a few seconds, you've taken a conversational breath and you've done a quick scan. You need only a second more for the last step, one that will give you the courage to say exactly what you need to say.

Your First Conversation Is a Small Talk

Leading up to my first trial as a young lawyer, the opposing counsel intimidated the heck out of me. He was respectful and nice enough, but he had thirty-plus years of experience. He knew he was good. And while I had confidence in my trial skills, I struggled to keep my mind sharp on the first day of arguments. I was nervous, and I rushed my words. During cross-examination, I focused on what I had to say next rather than using that moment to listen to the good information the witness was giving me.

I kicked myself—I knew exactly what I was doing

in the moment, but without pausing for a breath to collect my thoughts or allowing my awareness to guide me, I couldn't take control of the situation.

Driving home, I talked to myself out loud as I reflected on the highs and lows of the day. As I spoke, I started to cling to certain bite-size phrases that stuck out to me. I kept repeating them.

"You be Jefferson."

"Wait for the right pitch."

"Let the facts tell the truth."

These were the first of what I now call my small talks. They helped remind me to be myself, to wait for the weak spot in the witness's testimony, and to let the facts speak for themselves rather than try and do too much. I wrote these phrases at the top of my yellow legal pad the next morning. When I used my small talks, the difference in my demeanor and attitude in the courtroom was like night and day. I felt less insecure, more sure of myself. I didn't feel rushed. I didn't feel out of step.

Even now, I never go to trial without a small talk written at the top of my yellow pad.

Your mindset begins with your words. When you speak, your words don't just affect the other person. They also affect you. According to the latest studies in neuroscience and psychology, your language—that is, the actual words you use to form your thoughts—significantly influences your emotions and mindset, and eventually your reality.

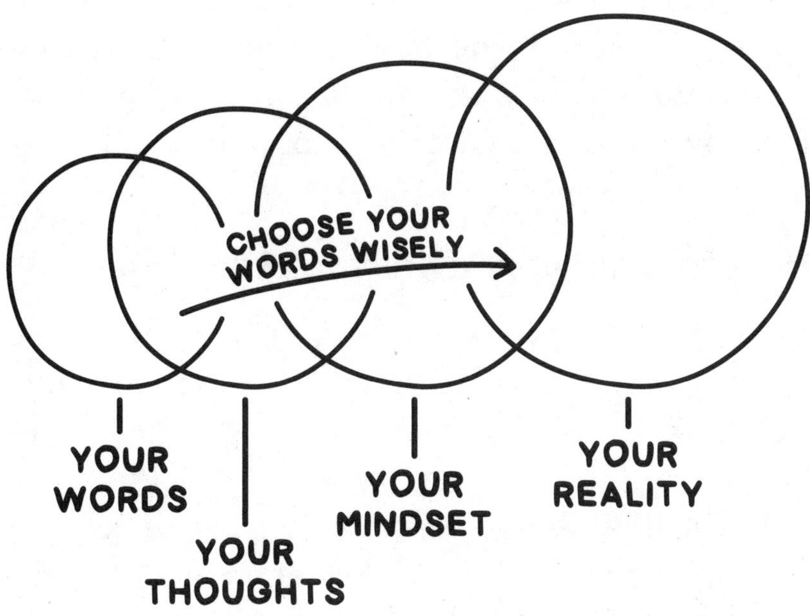

To build a mindset of confidence with my clients, I encourage them to use small talks. A small talk is just that: A small talk with yourself. A phrase that empowers you. A set of words that re-centers you when you feel off balance. It's like a positive affirmation. But whereas a positive affirmation typically includes an abstract statement of identity or self-empowerment like "I am loved" or "I am enough," a small talk is more concrete and tied to context, such as: "Start with my breath."

Small talks are powerful memory recall tools. They connect you to your desired mindset, whether it's to gain more confidence, prevent yourself from getting defensive, or remind yourself not to sweat the small stuff. Think of your small talk as your own mini-huddle with yourself, in which you call the play before you take the field.

How to build your own small talk

Building your own small talk is easier than you might think. There are, however, some guidelines to follow.

Tie your small talk to your goals

In chapter two, you learned the importance of understanding your goal and conversational values before engaging in difficult situations. When you tie your goal to your small talk, you put a belt and suspenders around the outcome you want in the interaction.

It's like doubling down on where you want the conversation to go. If your goal is to be confident, then build a small talk that reminds you to state your ideas and opinions confidently: "Voice it." Similarly, if your goal is to get through the conversation without arguing, then craft a small talk that reinforces that desired outcome: "Seek to understand." This phrase encourages active listening and empathy, focusing on understanding the other person's perspective rather than getting drawn into a conflict.

These goal-oriented small talks are personal cues or prompts that remind you of what you wish to achieve in the conversation, keeping you aligned with your overarching objectives. They help maintain focus and direction, especially in moments when it's easy to get sidetracked by emotions or opposing views.

Start with verbs

Instead of more general thoughts of identity, such as "I am strong" or "I am not my feelings," begin your small talk with a verb. The verb infuses action, creating active mindsets, like "Stand up" or "Feel, don't fixate."

When you use verbs, the small talks become sharper and more practical. The verb pushes you to act and behave, transforming what would be passive contemplation into active engagement. For instance, an affirmation like "My truth holds value" is passive. "Speak my truth" urges you to take immediate action, to vocalize your thoughts and beliefs. Similarly, a phrase like "Welcome the difficult" propels you forward, promoting an attitude of resilience and readiness to face obstacles head-on. If I had used a small talk with Bobby LaPray, it would've been "Find the struggle."

These verb-led phrases act as prompts for specific behaviors, encouraging you not just to think differently but to **do** differently. They create a sense of immediacy and urgency, making the small talk an effective tool for immediate behavioral change and self-empowerment.

Make it short and personal

Remember, your small talk isn't going to be plastered on a billboard. It doesn't need to resonate, much less be shared, with anyone other than you. Often, the best small talks are those that tie back to a personal experience or memory you want to recall or embody in the moment.

For example, I once had a client who wanted a present reminder to stay assertive when expressing her ideas at work. Her small talk?

"Tell 'em, Doris."

It was something her grandfather would playfully say to her grandmother when she started getting worked up about a topic she was passionate about. This simple phrase held a wealth of personal meaning and encouragement for my client. It reminded her of her grandmother's strength and assertiveness, inspiring her to channel the same energy.

It's a prime example of how a few words, deeply rooted in personal history, can serve as a powerful anchor in moments of self-doubt or hesitation. Small talks become more than just words; they are echoes of encouragement and resilience that resonate uniquely with the individual.

Improving your mindset starts with better selecting your words. You must choose words that treat you better. Words that serve you better. Words that move you forward regardless of past experiences that have held you back.

To illustrate, let's assume your small talk is "Stand firm." With this mindset, in a situation of disagreement, you're encouraged to select words that empower your autonomy in a positive way rather than push you down or leave you defeated. Here's what that contrast might sound like:

- Negative: "You're impossible."
- Positive: (Stand firm.) "I'm interested in a solution. If that's not on the table, tell me now."

- Negative: "I can't handle this."
- Positive: (Stand firm.) "I'm choosing to address this another time."

- Negative: "There's no point in trying."
- Positive: (Stand firm.) "I'm not going there with you."

Notice how the positive versions lead you to select words and phrases that treat you with respect and support your self-esteem. Take a moment to craft a small talk of your own. Remember, tie it to your goals, start with a verb, and make it personal to you. To inspire you, here's a quick list of effective small talks my clients have successfully used:

Confidence	"Keep your head up." "Shine anyway."

Assertiveness	"Claim your space." "Don't aggravate, articulate."
Defensiveness	"Put it down, [name]." "Let go, lean in."
Clarity	"Breathe in, breathe out." "Find the heart of it."
Calmness	"Slow down, [name]." "Use your anchor."

You can't control other people, but you can control the moment. The split second before a conversation begins is all the time you need. It's possibly the most powerful moment of a conversation, and most people don't even know it exists. Leverage that. Take a conversational breath. Do a quick scan. Have a small talk with yourself. You may be surprised at just how well the conversation turns out.

CHAPTER SUMMARY

- I'm giving you three tools to take more control over your communication: a conversational breath, a quick scan, and a small talk.

- A conversational breath gives you the benefits of slow, controlled breathing to keep your mind clear throughout an argument. Starting with an inhale through the nose, take a second sharp inhale, then a longer exhale, and keep a repeatable rhythm.

- A quick scan of your physical and mental state helps you release tension to stay calm and focused. Beginning with a conversational breath, close your eyes and examine where your stress is hiding in your body, then label what you're feeling.

- A small talk empowers you with a mindset that increases the feeling of control you have over your responses. Starting with a verb that pushes you to act, like **choose** or **stand**, create a short phrase that is meaningful to you and matches your values.

- Each of these three tools helps give you control in conflict by preventing you from unknowingly engaging your ignition phase.

CHAPTER 6

Control the Pace

"Sir, do you know approximately how fast you were going when the accident—"

"Maybe forty miles per hour," Chuck, my client, interrupted.

"—happened?" the other attorney finished, a hint of satisfaction in her voice. "I need you to let me get all of my question out first before you respond, okay?"

"Okay," he agreed.

"Do you know approximately how fast you were going when the accident happen—"

"About forty miles per hour," Chuck cut in again.

Again, the other attorney asked him for the space to finish her question. I became concerned. Attorneys want you to answer their questions quickly because it means you're not thinking about your answer. You become easier to control and susceptible to having words put in your mouth.

But Chuck knew better. We'd gone over the need to wait for the other attorney to get their full question on the record before answering, all part of our preparation for his deposition. He was starting to rush the tempo. I needed to get him out of his head. After the next question and answer, I asked for a quick break to speak with Chuck in the hallway.

As we walked out of the room, I motioned with my yellow notepad to some chairs in the corner. "Let's go take a seat over there," I said.

"Okay," he said, almost panting.

After we sat down, I asked nonchalantly, "So what are you going to do this weekend? Any plans?"

He looked puzzled. "Huh?"

"This weekend," I repeated while unwrapping a peppermint. "What do y'all have going on?"

"Oh. Uh, I'm not sure, let me think." As he thought, he went quiet. I saw his shoulders lower. His breathing slowed down. After seven seconds or so, he responded, "We're taking the kids to see that movie about the talking animals."

"The new one that just came out?" I asked.

He gave another short pause. "Yep, that's the one."

"Hey, that'll be fun," I said. "What are their ages again?"

"Five and seven," he said with a smile, now relaxed. The reset worked.

"Awesome ages," I said, standing up no sooner than we had sat down. He stood up too. "Listen," I told him, "when you go back in there, I want you to treat each question like she's asking you what you're going to do this weekend. Answer just like you did with me. Take your moment."

Chuck nodded; the analogy clicked. "Got it. Pause, right. Let it breathe."

"Exactly," I said. "You control the pace. Not her."

When we walked back into the deposition room, the difference was night and day. He never stepped on a question again, each time taking his moment to consider his answer. The hurried, almost panicked energy had gone away, replaced by a calm, deliberate presence. The opposing attorney noticed the change too, her rhythm disrupted by Chuck's composure. She wasn't able to rush him with rapid-fire questions. He did great.

The Gift of a Pause

When you're anxious, scared, or upset, do you talk faster or slower?

You talk **faster**.

It's a sign of your ignition phase, and it's normal. The increased heart rate speeds up your thought processes, readying you for split-second reactions. Reflexes become quicker. Speed becomes the priority. As a result, your mind starts to think faster than your mouth can often get out the words. That's why you tend to speak much faster than you normally would. The desire to rush causes you to emotionally react rather than logically respond. You may be familiar with the more technical phrase: putting your foot in your mouth.

When you rush, you not only expose yourself to the obvious issues like stumbling over your words and leaving thoughts half-expressed, but you also rush your point. You miss the chance to fully develop your position. Rushing your words also signals that you're not really listening, instead conveying that you were already planning out your sentence before hearing the other person's words. You miss things.

In these types of scenarios where you feel yourself speeding up, there's a misplaced belief that you have zero control over it. That you're simply along for the ride. But the truth is that your foot is on the brake the whole time.

You just need to push.

In addition to the tools that you learned in the prior chapter, there's one piece of your communication that will separate you from the rest.

A well-timed pause.

Silence may be the absence of sound, but it's not the absence of communication. I mean it when I say this: silence is **the** most effective tool at your disposal to fix communication problems.

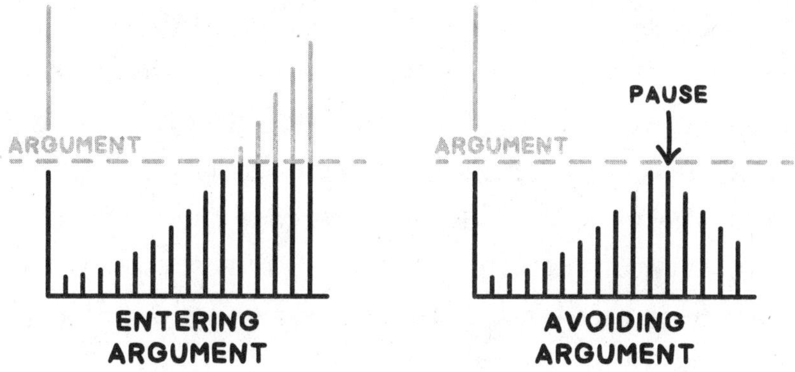

Why don't more people use it? The issue is twofold. For one, many people avoid silence because they don't see it as optimal. Part of that thought comes from the standard of speed in communication you see in modern media. Podcast and social media clips are edited down to remove pauses. Movies and television shows often dramatize the impact of quick dialogue, making it seem as though everyone already knows what they're going to say. Well, that's because actors have the benefit of a written script and film editors. It's not real-life communication. Take the talking heads on the nightly news as another example. Outlets tend to showcase opposing viewpoints, whether that's in politics or sports, through quick retorts or "clapbacks," as if they're the pinnacle of intellectual victory. It has the effect of skewing perception that speed is preferred over substance. Arguments in the real world don't happen like they do in the media. It's not a healthy metric.

Second, people tend to fear that silence shows weakness. In more professional environments, for instance, there's a pervasive thought that not responding immediately to questions, whether in email or in person, demonstrates a lack of knowledge or preparation. That fear drives you to prioritize immediacy, sometimes at the expense of accuracy or thoughtfulness. In everyday conversations too, you may find yourself using verbal fillers to fill the silence with speech (think "you know") or sound (think "uh" and "um"). There's a sense that silence conveys incompetence, when in reality, silence is wisdom in waiting. It's rushing your words that shows weakness. Slowing your words shows strength.

By understanding how to use pauses, you enhance your image of competence and show that you're someone who is more deliberate and therefore more credible. Rather than thinking that silence shows uncertainty, take the mindset that silence ensures what follows **is certain.** The strategic use of silence reflects intention, not hesitation. When well timed, pauses are a sign of confidence and self-control. More often than not, the person who controls the pace of the conversation is the person most in control of themselves.

That's what's so powerful about a pause. It gifts you with the ability to control **time.**

Here's what that control over time provides you with:

Time to reflect. Pauses give you space to choose. It's a mindset that no one can make you say anything that you don't want to say. You can choose to respond if you wish, sure. But you can also choose to say nothing. No response is still a response. You have the choice, always. Pauses give you time not just to choose your words, but to own them. When you pause, you're not only controlling the conversation's pace. You're affirming your presence in it.

This time to reflect isn't about hesitation—it's about deliberate acknowledgment that you know who you are. When you pause before responding, it demonstrates that you are in control of your emotions and thoughts. You're showing the other person that you're not swayed by impulse but guided by thoughtfulness. Every time you hold back words, you're putting your value, your confidence, and your power on display.

Pauses give you the power to choose and decide:

- Is this person worth my peace of mind?
- Is what I want to say something that needs to be said? Does it need to be said now? And am I the one to say it?
- Will my words help or hurt the conversation?
- Am I speaking to provide value, or just speaking to hear myself?

- Will my words make progress toward my goals and values?
- Is there more I need to understand before I respond?

Words that come after a deliberate choice of silence have more impact because they indicate that what follows has been measured, adding weight to your meaning.

Time to reconsider. A pause gives you time to compose your behavior, as with a conversational breath, a quick scan, or a small talk. It provides an assessment of your readiness to be present in the moment. It preserves your energy, like a rest between sets during a hard workout. The use of silence is also critical to evaluating the world around you. You can read the room. You get the chance to observe their reactions, expressions, and body language. By pausing, you're taking the other person's temperature. It pulls you out of only focusing on what you're trying to say and instead puts your five senses to work on first figuring out what they're trying to tell you.

It's the difference between running into conflict bullheaded versus having the wherewithal to say to yourself, **Wait, is this really what I want to say?** A pause allows you to step back and consider whether the direction of the conversation is aligning with your desired goals and values for the conversation.

The external observation that a pause allows informs and guides you in how to proceed—whether to soften your approach, reaffirm your stance, or introduce a new angle.

Time to regulate. When things start to get heated in conversation, silence serves as a wet blanket. It puts distance between the stimulus and the response, reducing the intensity of rising emotions. It allows fires to burn out. That's why silence is crucial to getting to the cooling point. It allows you to recalibrate your tone. A pause makes the strategic choice to avoid saying something that could make matters worse. It shows maturity and wisdom. It puts you as the bigger person. You get to decide when there's been enough said. You get to decide when you're done, rather than it ending on their terms.

And not only does a pause help you regulate your own emotions, but it also helps the other person reflect on theirs. It breaks the cycle of rapid response, preventing both of you from losing your cooling phases. That's a big deal. Pauses keep arguments more fractured because they prevent the back-and-forth rhythm that quickly ramps up tension. That's a good thing. They keep both of you from "flooding" because you're inserting space in between to keep yourselves clearheaded.

Don't allow the misconceptions of silence to keep you from accepting the power of your pause. Use it to control time in your favor, creating opportunities for meaningful thought and contemplation in every conversation.

How and When to Use Pauses

If you want to speak with more control, you have to be more comfortable with silence. There's no getting around it. What will you say with yours?

The silence of a pause does communicate something. Again, it may be the absence of sound, but it's not the absence of communication. Consider the different messages and signals that can be sent by a pause:

- A pause after the first time he says, "I love you."
- A pause after she asks, "Do you like my new dress?"
- A pause after everyone yells, "Surprise!"
- A pause after she asks, "Where were you last night?"

What a pause says to someone is largely determined by how long it is. For example, if I don't respond to your text within five minutes, typically it's no problem. But five days? Then I communicate something else.

In the following pages, I've outlined this distinction and how you can best take advantage of the unique strengths of a pause depending on how long you let the silence last, turning each moment of quiet into a powerful tool for communication.

Short pauses are reading glasses

A short pause is between one and four seconds. Short pauses bring emphasis and focus on specific words, like putting on a pair of glasses to read the fine print. You see the words better.

Short pauses convey that what you're about to say has been thought about. That you've taken time to weigh and measure your words.

For example, imagine that someone in the office asks you, "Will you have that report back by this afternoon?" A short pause changes your sense of control:

- Without a pause, you snap back, "I've already said that I won't."
- After a four-second pause, you slowly respond, "I've already said that I won't."

Did the voice in your head read that same phrase differently the second time? With just a few seconds of silence, you sound firmer. More sure of yourself.

Let's try an even simpler one. This time, imagine a friend asks you, "How are you doing?" Again, watch the contrast in tone.

- Without a pause, you quip, "I'm good."
- After a three-second pause, you reply, "I'm good."

Did you hear it? The immediate answer conveys that you hardly put any thought into what you said, almost dismissive or flippant. It may have even sounded less genuine. Add a pause, however, and it shows that you thought about your answer. And that gives your answer more force and effect. You know that you're good.

Short pauses are great for answering normal questions, especially if you're in an interview or deposition situation. I tell my clients to add a few seconds of silence after the questions and before their responses. Remember, **your first word is your breath**. Not only does it give you time to consider and replay their question in your mind, but what you say comes out more controlled.

A short pause is also good for adding emphasis, such as pausing before a punch line or just the right . . . word. The silence grabs attention like a cliffhanger. It sparks curiosity about what you will say next.

It's another reason why a conversational breath is so crucial—it's a short pause. Normally, when you talk, you breathe in on the inhale and speak on the exhale. The inhale of a conversational breath is three seconds total, which is just enough time to allow you to realign yourself to center and speak with a controlled, even tone on the exhale.

The person who pauses before responding—whether it's in the classroom, boardroom, or living room—will almost always come across as more controlled and confident.

Long pauses are mirrors

A long pause is anywhere between five and ten seconds. Any longer than that and it's not a pause. It's a time-out.

Unlike short pauses for focus, long pauses are for reflection. Like a two-sided mirror. Long pauses not only allow you to reflect on your response, but more important, they force the other person to look back at themselves at the same time.

When someone is rude to you, insults you, or belittles you, a long pause is your greatest weapon. Here's why:

1. Five to ten seconds of silence gives enough time for their words to echo back to them. The sound of their comment will linger in the air and will often make them question or doubt their message. That's why sometimes someone will use this silence to preemptively say, "I'm sorry," or "I shouldn't have said that," before you need to respond.

2. Silence can never be misquoted. It's far better to respond with nothing than with something hurtful that is sure to go down

in your relationship history book to be cited again and again when problems reappear.

3. The person who speaks last often loses. In negotiations, they say the person to speak first loses. But in arguments, it's the opposite. Why? Because the only way to beat someone saying hurtful things is to say something more hurtful. The only way to outdo someone's cutting comment is to cut deeper. When you force yourself to have the last word, you'll likely be the one expected to apologize first. By inserting a long pause, stopping yourself from having the last say, you leave the other person's words exposed.

Long pauses work particularly well with people who aren't telling you the truth.

As you can imagine, as a trial attorney, I've heard a lot of witnesses lie. You become so used to it that you really don't get surprised anymore when people lie to you. Even under oath.

In this one particular case, during a deposition, I knew the witness was lying to me.

I knew he was lying because I had the evidence. He was an eighteen-wheeler driver who had crashed into my client and blamed the wreck on another vehicle. The driver's cell phone records showed that he had sent a text from his phone at the exact same time as the accident, as well as other texts leading up to the wreck. But he didn't know that I had them.

"Were you texting while driving?" I asked point-blank.

"Nope," he answered firmly. "I never text when I'm driving."

His first mistake, using an absolute. **Never.** When someone uses an absolute, they typically walk themselves out on a plank. So if they're going to say never, it had better be never.

I used a long pause, about eight seconds, while his words lingered.

His eyes began to dart around the table. He started to shift his weight in his seat. Having had enough time to hear his words echo back to him, he broke the silence and changed what he had just said. "I mean, I say never. I guess sometimes I do. I mean, it just depends on the situation, you know. I honestly don't remember."

His second mistake. He started to back out of his answer—in Texas, we call that **crawfishin'**.

I gave it another long pause. This time, ten seconds. Enough to make it almost uncomfortable.

Honest people don't mind the discomfort of a pause. It's in the silence that honest people know their truth has no need to hide. Dishonest people, on the other hand, typically can't stand it. It's in the silence that dishonest people feel as if they have everything to prove. They sense you're not taking the bait. They'll fill the space for you, having conversations in their head about what you're thinking or going to say. They often unravel their own stories in their eagerness to fill the void.

Sensing his retreat, I gave him a choice: come back to the truth or walk off the plank.

I repeated my original question. "Were you texting while driving?"

"I might've been, yeah," he said, sounding almost relieved.

I put my hand on a folder of papers next to me at the table. It was just a stack of other documents. The actual cell phone records were still in my bag.

With my hand still on the folder, I pressed him: "You were texting your coworker."

He nodded, and said, "Yeah."

In only a few minutes, he had made a full 180-degree turn. No arguments. No yelling. No shouting, "You can't handle the truth!" All I had done was use the power of a long pause. He saw how his words looked in the mirror and did the rest.

In chapter eight, I'm going to teach you how to refine your pause techniques to most effectively respond to those who say things to hurt you. For now, all you need to know is that different situations call for different pauses. Whether you're dealing with a direct confrontation, navigating a tricky professional conversation, or simply engaging in a deep, personal dialogue, the right pause at the right time can transform the dynamics of the exchange to put you in control.

It's about more than just silence. It's about controlling time to slow down your reactions and build space for reflection, reconsideration, and regulation.

CHAPTER SUMMARY

- A well-timed pause credits you with the power of time. Time to reflect, time to reconsider, and time to regulate.

- Pausing in an argument isn't a sign of hesitation. It's a sign of intention and self-control. More often than not, the person who controls the pace of the conversation is the person most in control of themself.

- Words that come after a deliberate choice of silence have more impact because they indicate that what follows has been measured, adding weight to the meaning.

- The length of a pause is useful for different contexts. A short pause of one to four seconds before responding or answering a question makes you sound stronger and more resolute. A longer pause of five to ten seconds creates anticipation and serves as a mirror that engages the cooling phase.

- When you embrace the silence of a pause, you take control of the speed of a conflict. It's like using the brakes on a car: controlling the speed of the interactions lets you safely steer it toward a more constructive outcome.

Rule 2:
Say It with Confidence

CHAPTER 7

Assertive Voice

You're a volunteer test subject in a study on feelings. Doctors attach all sorts of sticky pads and wires to your head and chest to monitor your vitals. One scientist walks up to you with his wooden clipboard and notepad. He demands, "Feel happy right this instant."

You give him a puzzled look. **Feel happy? About what?** Sure, you try on a fake smile and force some laughter, but it's far from the real thing. You try to think of something to be happy about. But it's just not working.

The scientist scribbles on his notepad. Then he demands, "Feel scared right this instant."

Just like last time, you struggle to feel scared. Admittedly, all the wires and monitors are sort of weird, but you're not truly scared. You try to recall the last scary movie you saw, but your mind wanders and you think about the fact that world news is scarier than most movies.

The scientist writes down more notes. This time, the scientist takes in a big breath and instructs you, "Feel mad right this instant." But as soon as the word **instant** comes out of his mouth—**whop!**—he slams his clipboard on the top of your head.

Immediately, your eyebrows shoot down as you give him a look. **I know you didn't just do what I think you did.** You're shocked and offended. Most of all, you instantly feel **mad.**

The scientist smiles. "Now feel forgiveness!"

Confidence Is a Feeling

"Jefferson, how do I feel confident?"

Whether it's about navigating the workplace, acing an interview, or speaking up for yourself, it's by far the most-asked question I receive. It's also the wrong question to ask.

Feelings can't be flipped on like a light switch. They come from something, like a bad memory, a happy thought, or a stressful environment. They arise for a reason, like a hit on the head. Confidence works the same way. Confidence is a **feeling.** It can't be summoned at will. You can't call it off the bench. That's why it's often not there when you need it. You know confidence when you feel confidence. It's the ability to operate under a feeling of knowledge and appreciation for your strengths as well as your limits.

So, to ask "How do I feel confident?" is like asking "How do I feel mad?" It doesn't work like that. The only way to feel more confident is to live it out more fully. Confidence is an active process that you build and accumulate by engaging in specific behaviors.

The question isn't "How do I feel confident?" The question is "What can I do to create experiences that build my confidence?" Confidence is found in the doing. And that doing is called assertiveness. Confidence is as assertive does.

Assertiveness is how you express confidence. Unlike confidence, which is a feeling, asserting is an action. You can think of it as confidence is an inside thing, while assertiveness is an outside thing. To assert yourself is confidence in motion. Assertiveness is found in the way you say things, the way you lean into your words.

Confidence and assertiveness feed into each other. Together, the pair creates a positive feedback loop: speaking more assertively produces the feeling of confidence, while the feeling of newfound confidence emboldens you to speak more assertively. It's a life-changing combo. To be able to stand up for your needs and opinions in a way that gains you credibility rather than takes it away is a power beyond words.

How do you speak assertively? I'll show you.

But this isn't something to read once and expect that you'll magically remember it when you need it. Rather, take one of the following ten lessons and apply it to your **next conversation**.

Your assertiveness training starts now.

Don't make me get my clipboard.

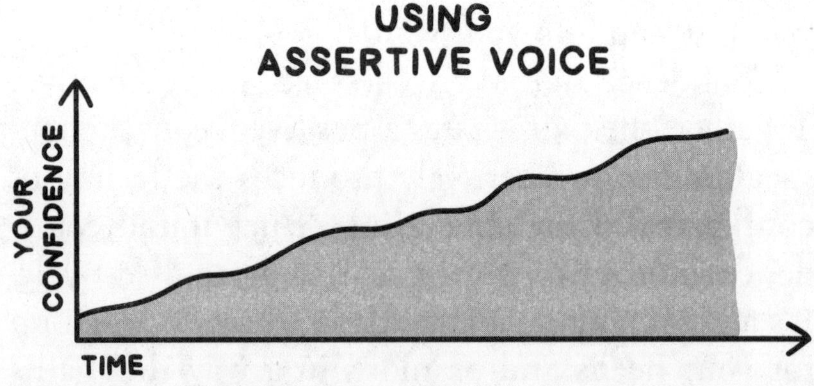

10 Ways to Practice Assertiveness Now

Assertiveness begins with the basics. You'll start by building a vocabulary of assertive words and commonly used phrases that conveys confidence without aggression. Then, you'll learn the particular sound and intonation patterns that embody self-respect. In conversations, emails, texts, and videoconferences, you'll begin to spot the opportunities to stand your ground with firm kindness. Soon enough, you'll find yourself fully immersed in the language of assertiveness, and before you know it, you'll feel confident in any conversation without a second thought.

Let's begin.

Lesson 1: Every word matters

Above all the tips and tricks about how to be more assertive, nothing matters more than word choice. The language you choose—each and every word you select—directly impacts your ability to assert yourself. Every email you write, every text you send.

Every.

Word.

Matters.

As I asked at the start of this book: Who do your words say you are? Actions often speak louder than words, but they're not a replacement. There's power in a spoken word. Your words are your personality, your reputation, and your character. Investing in your words and phrasing is investing in your future self—your self-esteem and the person you want to be. For example, imagine a simple email to a coworker:

- "I just wanted to touch base on the outline."

Now, let's adjust one word:

- "I wanted to touch base on the outline."

Do you sense the difference? One sentence signals caution. The other builds confidence. With one word removed, the sentence takes on a new voice. The first sentence, with **just**, sounds almost hesitant, as if you don't mean to bother them (even though you do). The second sentence asserts exactly what you want to do.

Here are a few more before-and-afters:

- Unsure: "I'm sort of wondering if I should maybe ask the team."
- Assertive: "I'll ask the team."

- Unsure: "I guess I'm just looking for a bit more clarity on your expectations."
- Assertive: "I need more clarity on your expectations."

What assertiveness requires isn't difficult. You can do this. You **know** this. You have all the skills already inside you to unlock a new voice. Once you begin to open your eyes to the everyday uncertain language used in your communication as well as in others', wasted words will start to stick out to you like sore thumbs. You'll never be able to unsee them.

Lesson 2: Prove it to yourself

Confidence is found in the doing, remember? To feel confident, you need to begin proving to yourself that you'll do what you say you'll do. That means you'll inform the other person of your next step, then you'll take it. The key is to say it out loud. Say what you're doing, or going to do, out loud and in the present tense. For example:

- "I'm moving forward from this conversation."
- "I'm asking for your permission."
- "I'm setting a reminder."

It's **not** "I kind of" or "I sort of" or "I guess." Take out the hesitation by voicing your actions and intentions.

Here's another that I see all the time in emails:

- "Please see the attached."

What does that even mean? Of course they're going to see it. You put it in the email. Of course they know it's attached. They can see the attachment. **Please** doesn't add any value. This phrasing is passive and weak, as if you have no role in it. Maybe it doesn't bother you. But why pass over even the smallest opportunity to demonstrate confidence in your communication, credibility, or reputation?

"I'm attaching the contract," or even "I attached the contract," sounds more forward, more active, and more assertive. You're leaning into your confidence by telling them what you're doing and then doing it.

The effect of telling the other person what you're going to do is secondary to the major effect it has on you. There is a sense of empowerment you'll receive when you claim your words and see them through to fulfillment, like telling yourself, "Hey, I've got this." You're proving to yourself that you believe in your own abilities—small, assertive actions that accumulate into experiences that build your confidence. These steps make even bigger impacts when it comes to enforcing boundaries, as you'll learn in chapter nine. By telling people what you're going to do and then doing it, you're proving that you're the kind of person who, when you say something, you mean it. Otherwise, you're bound to get walked over.

Imagine that you're in a heated argument. The exchange has escalated to the point where the personal attacks intensify, and you feel the need to disengage. In a high pitch you shout, "I swear if you say that one more time, I'm leaving! I'm so over this, I mean it!" Without hesitation, the other person says it again. But you **don't leave.** You stay, continuing to argue and yell, exacerbating the situation.

Did you build your credibility or take away from it?

What's worse, you undermined yourself. Now, the other person knows that you're not serious. You've established a baseline that you're all bark and no bite.

Take back control with assertive language and lean in. Tell them what you're going to do, then do it:

- Instead of abruptly leaving and slamming the door, say, "I'm going to leave the room"—and then do so.
- Instead of suddenly hanging up the phone, say, "I'm going to end the call"—and then do so.

Think of it like calling your shot in a game of pool. Acting in line with your aim demonstrates self-assurance. You're conveying that you're not afraid to state your intention. You believe in your ability to deliver. And when you follow through, you solidify that belief. This consistency is part of the positive feedback loop, in which you say what you're going to do and you do it. And you'll feel more confident the next go-around.

Confidence is showing up and proving to yourself that you'll be there when you say you will. When you honor your self-promises, meet your own expectations, and use assertive language, you will increase your ability to rely on yourself.

Lesson 3: Express your needs unapologetically

Imagine that you're the best lawyer in the world. You're wearing professional clothes and exuding confidence. Your client is the real you, in plain clothes, as if you've made a current duplicate of yourself with all your same wants, needs, and worries. You're in a big corporate room where other people sit at the table opposite you and your client. You pat your client on the shoulder and tell them to take a seat while you remain standing.

In this moment, you know that if you don't speak up for your client, nobody else will. You are your client's only hope. You're prepared, and you understand exactly what your client wants. As the meeting begins, you speak out on behalf of your client:

- "My client won't accept that."
- "My client wants fair expectations."
- "My client needs assurance this won't happen again."

As you stick up for your client, you sound strong. You sound assertive. You're not just participating; you're leading the conversation with confidence, fiercely advocating for your client's needs and rights. Every word you choose is deliberate, aiming to protect and promote your client's best interests and ensuring that your client is treated with the dignity they deserve. And as you do, you realize the power of your voice.

Now, with the same power and tone, the same sense of justice, replace **my client** with **I**.

- "I won't accept that."
- "I want fair expectations."
- "I need assurance this won't happen again."

That's advocating for yourself.

To be more assertive, set your default to stating your needs. Begin sentences with "I need." This simple shift in language empowers you to take ownership of your wants and to communicate them clearly.

- "I need a moment."
- "I need to speak with you."
- "I need you to know how that affected me."
- "I need your help."

You can't speak assertively without knowing how to assert your needs. You have to be your own advocate. That means you're going to stop over-apologizing. No, not the real apologies. I'm talking about the fake ones, the unnecessary ones, the ones that don't mean anything. The **I'm sorrys** that you litter onto your requests, questions, or clarifications, like:

- "Hey, I'm so sorry, do you have a quick minute?"
- "No, I can't today. I'm sorry!"
- "So sorry to bother you."
- "Sorry, I'm not sure I understand."
- "I'm sorry, can you repeat that?"

The word **sorry** might feel safe, but it does more harm than good for your self-esteem. Save the real **I'm sorrys** for when it matters, like asking for forgiveness, owning up to a mistake, or sympathizing with someone else's pain.

Instead of over-apologizing, use words of gratitude, or nothing at all.

- Before: "Sorry I'm late."
- After: "Thank you for your patience."[1]

- Before: "Sorry to bother you."
- After: "I appreciate your help."

- Before: "Sorry for all the questions."
- After: "Thank you for clarifying that for me."

---

1. Unless you're really late, in which case you should apologize.

Whether you realize it or not, over-apologizing takes a toll on your mindset. You'll see yourself more as a nuisance or annoyance. Know this: your self-worth isn't tied to how little an inconvenience you can be. Asserting your needs and voicing them in a way that maintains respect and credibility is never inconvenient—it's necessary.

Lesson 4: Speak when it matters

At my prior law firm, I was in a heated partners' meeting discussing typical end-of-year topics like bonuses, salary raises, and next-year initiatives. Every time progress seemed to be made, it never failed: one person found a way to make a comment or poke holes in whatever was being proposed. This person did so regardless of whether the comment was relevant, derailing the decision and prolonging the meeting. I'm all in favor of a devil's advocate on ideas, but this person relished highlighting "but what if" problems without any interest in taking ownership of the solutions.

You know the type. This person would audibly complain about how stressed they were while also working the least. It was open knowledge that this person had the fewest hours and billings of everyone at the table. The least amount of grip on the pulse of the firm and its direction. The person was "all hat and no cattle," a Texan way of saying they're all talk, no action. The more this person spoke, the more respect and credibility they lost. With each chime-in, more people groaned, sighed, or rolled their eyes.

The most valued senior partner, however, hardly spoke. When this partner did, though, everyone stopped and paid attention. The silence wasn't due to a lack of interest but rather an understanding of when this partner's voice was needed.

It's frequently the person who knows the least, has contributed the least, or whose opinion matters the least who has the most to say. I'm sure you've been in a virtual meeting where the least-informed person is typically the one who feels the urge to put in their two cents toward every minor issue.

One of the biggest separators between those who show confidence and those who don't is how often they feel the need to say something. It's a dead giveaway. I'm not saying that you shouldn't chime in, express concern, or be a team player. The point I'm making is that insecure people often have the urge to say **everything**. Their insecurity convinces them that they have everything to prove. Everyone must know how smart they are, how right they are, how "better than you" they are. The fact that they feel unsure of themselves drives their desire to make certain that you think they aren't. This insecurity manifests in apparent ways: name-dropping, one-upping, or an insistence on having the last word.

Confident people have the urge to say **nothing**. There is wisdom in their silence. They're listening.

They're observing, absorbing. Confident people know that they have nothing to prove because they have an assurance in their abilities and knowledge. They trust themselves without regard to external validation. Because they feel sure of themselves, there's no desire to seek the limelight.

If an insecure person can't feel confident about their contribution, they'll choose to feel confident in their criticism. Don't be that person. And the next time you see it, understand that they're scratching their insecurity itch. Let it be a reminder that true confidence chooses the moment of input.

Lesson 5: Say less

The fewer the words, the clearer the point.

Think of conversation like supply and demand. Economics says that when you have too much of something, people want it less. The oversupply decreases the price. Conversely, where there is too little of something, people want it more. The demand drives the price up. The same principle applies to communication. The more words you use, the less I want to listen and the less value your words have. But the fewer words you use, the more I want to pay attention and the more value each word holds. Each word has impact. When you flood the market of conversation with excessive words, you create a deficit of attention.

This is also why overexplaining kills confidence.

The more words you use, the less you actually say. Using too many words to say something small creates a big problem. The temptation to overexplain stems from the fear that the other person isn't going to believe you (a social evaluation trigger). But the more words you use, the less believable you sound. The more words it takes to tell the truth, the more it sounds like a lie. The longer you talk, the more it sounds like you don't know what you're talking about.

Lesson 6: Remove filler words

You know them as the **ums**, **ahs**, and **uhs** that delay your speech. Fillers are natural and common. They're mostly used subconsciously as a way to fill the gaps of silence and keep up the sound of conversation. In an informal setting with friends and family, they're no issue. Simple filler words can help maintain the flow of conversation. You don't even really hear them because you're relaxing and relating on a deeper level. But in a more formal or professional setting, they signal hesitation and water down your confidence. Verbal crutches convey that you're not prepared or that you're less confident about what you're saying.

Some filler words you may not even notice:

- "Like"
- "You know?" or "You know what I mean?"

- "Right?" or "I know, right?"
- "So, yeah"

Instead, simply replace your fillers with **silence**. Notice the difference:

- Before: "So, yeah, um, like, okay, you know how when you talk with fillers, they sort of, like, distract from, like, your message, right?"
- After: "When you talk with fillers, they distract from your message."

See? Even trying to read the before passage, you can't quickly ascertain what it's saying. Fix it by embracing the silence.

When you first try this method, you will likely speak more slowly because you're putting intention into the next word to prevent a filler from taking its place. That's okay. Resist the urge to fill the air with noise. Get comfortable with silence.

As you learned in chapter six, silence adds pauses and gives you better control. It presents you with the option to add emphasis. In your head, using this method may feel awkward or weird. But to the listener, you sound intentional and confident with your words. Filler words add no value to the listener. Every unnecessary word detracts from your message.

Remove the words that water down your sentences. If you want to sound assertive, serve your words neat.

Lesson 7: Never undersell

If you don't believe your words have value, neither will the other person. Using phrases that undervalue your worth will slowly eat away at your confidence. Phrases like:

- "I hate to bother you."
- "I know this might sound stupid."
- "Forgive me for the dumb question."
- "I'm probably missing something here."
- "You probably know better than me."

Listen. I understand that you saying these things comes from a good place—I do. You want to soften your approach, almost in a humble, self-deprecating tone. And that's admirable. But it's not often received that way by the listener.

Instead, the signal you're sending is that you see yourself as less. It sounds more like you're hedging to lower their expectations of your contribution. It casts a shadow of doubt over your capabilities before you've even fully shared them.

As a result, the other person will associate these words with your actual impact and influence. That is, when you say, "I hate to bother you," what the other person hears is: "What I'm about to tell you **will** bother you." Or that what you're about to say will sound stupid, or the question you're about to ask is dumb. None of these messages are assertive. It's similar to the discussion about over-apologizing. It's like you're apologizing for taking up space, which is the exact opposite of assertive language. When you use these sorts of phrases, you also put a social obligation on the other person to relieve or forgive you by saying, "Oh, you're not bothering me," or "It's not a dumb question." It forces the two of you to have a mini conversation about your insecurity before you even get to your point. By framing your interactions with an undersell, you inadvertently reinforce the idea that your voice is not worth hearing, or is worth less than others'.

You also undersell yourself when you add the phrase "Does that make sense?" after your sentence. I understand that it comes from a need to feel assured that what you said came across the right way, that you're seeking validation that what you said actually made sense. But in reality, the phrase sets you up for a lose-lose situation. At best, it makes you sound like you're unsure of yourself. Like you don't believe in what you said. For example, "I was thinking we could move tomorrow's meeting due to the weather, with traffic and all. Does that make sense?" And at worst, you risk offending your listener, because it assumes that they may not have understood what you said, when they definitely did. For instance, "So you just connect these two parts here and it'll start working. Does that make sense?" To prevent either of these undesirable outcomes, it's best to totally omit the question or replace it with "What are your thoughts?" or "How does that sound?"

Every time you catch yourself about to downplay your presence, pause and reconsider how you can phrase your thoughts assertively, without the sound of self-doubt. Remember, your contributions are valuable, and expressing them confidently can change not only how others perceive you but also how you perceive yourself.

So instead, focus on phrasing that builds upon or breaks down the issue being raised. For example:

- "I'd like to build upon what you said."
- "I'd like to dig a bit deeper."
- "Can I take that a bit further?"
- "I have some insight that might add value here."

These phrases sound more like you're leaning into your question or point of view rather than shying away from it.

Lesson 8: Cut the excess

One of the quickest ways to boost your assertive vocabulary is to cut adverbs from your sentences. Adverbs are words that modify verbs or adjectives.

You most likely know them as words that end in **-ly** or express a certain degree.

- Just
- So
- Very
- Actually
- Basically
- Essentially
- Literally

I'm not saying these words are bad, and they're **just** fine in casual conversation. But if you want to speak more assertively when it matters, and you understand that every word matters, adverbs can go out the window. Compare, "So essentially, adverbs can actually dilute your sentences," with "Adverbs dilute your sentences."

A lot of other phrases clutter your assertiveness. See if any of these examples ring a bell:

- "What I'm saying is . . ." or "All I'm saying is . . ."
- "I just find it funny how . . ."
- "No offense, but . . ."
- "It's just that . . ."
- "I mean . . ."
- "I just need to say . . ."
- "To be honest . . ."
- "Don't take this the wrong way . . ."

- "I just really . . ."
- "I'm just curious . . ."
- "So I'm thinking maybe like . . ."

At best, these phrases undermine your credibility, and at worst, they're disingenuous. Cut them; you don't need them. Instead, say everything **after** the adverb you want to use.

Lesson 9: When in doubt, fall back on experience

Often, particularly in the workplace, you'll be asked a question that you don't know the answer to. When that happens, how you respond gives you an opportunity to use assertive language. Rather than putting on a deer-in-the-headlights look, rely on your past experiences:

- "I haven't come across this before."
- "In my experience . . ."
- "In the past, I've . . ."
- "From what I've seen . . ."

Relying on your past gives you a more solid foundation for responding, even when you don't know the immediate answer. Mind you, there's nothing wrong with saying, "I don't know." In fact, admitting ignorance is a sign of honesty and humility that can build trust. Following that admission with a commitment to find out or a reflection on a relevant experience demonstrates your dedication to providing value. Rather than throwing your hands up in the air, falling back on your past experiences shows that you're proactive, leveraging your knowledge to navigate uncertainties.

Lesson 10: Say "I'm confident"

This lesson is easy. Before you give your answer, begin with the phrase "I'm confident." It doesn't much matter what you say after it. The listener hears the word **confident** and associates that behavior with you.

- Before: "**I think** my skills will be an asset to your company."
- After: "**I'm confident** my skills will be an asset to your company."

- Before: "**I believe** I can help."
- After: "**I'm confident** I can help."

- Before: "**I guess** if I have questions, I know where to look."
- After: "**I'm confident** that if I have questions, I know where to look."

Again, think about your own response when another person uses the phrase **I think** versus **I'm confident**. Which person do you trust more?

Mind Your Tone

As I said at the outset of this book, it's not what you say, it's how you say it. If I tell you only what words to use and not how they sound, I'm not keeping my promise. What exactly does confidence **sound** like?

It's a balance. I imagine hearing music through a pair of headphones, when it isn't too loud in either ear. The sound is balanced. In assertive communication, the balance says, "I respect you, and I respect myself." That's the difference between assertiveness and aggressiveness. Aggressive communication doesn't care about respecting the other person. Assertive communication does. The sound is a steady, even tone. You let your words carry the sentence, implying both conviction and expectation.

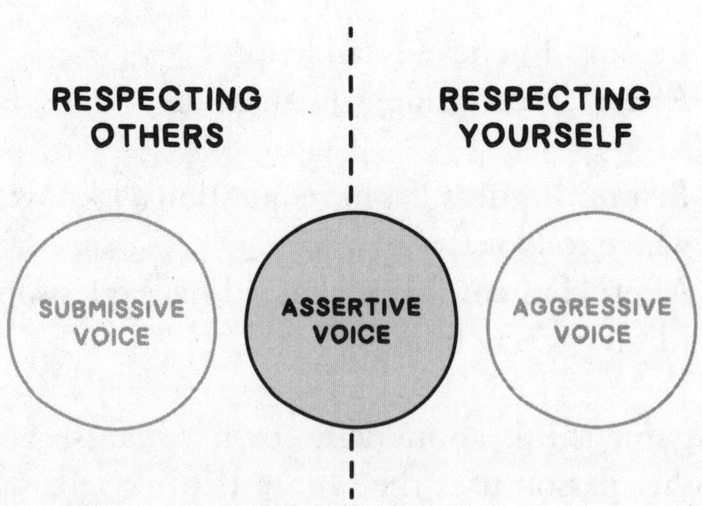

A key here is to avoid uptalk, the tendency to tilt your words with an upward inflection at the end. It's a rising intonation, the kind you use when you're asking a question, like "Are you sure?" The sound suggests uncertainty, or a request for approval, even when the statements are declarative.

To sound more confident, end your sentences with a downward or neutral inflection. Think of it as asking a family member to pass the salt while you're eating dinner. You wouldn't use uptalk and say, "Can you please pass the salt?" as if you don't know what salt is or doubt their ability to pass it. You most likely use a neutral tone, more akin to a statement, where your tone doesn't rise but stays the same.

Eye contact is another vital component of assertive communication. It signals engagement, sincerity, and confidence. In a meeting, when you're sharing an idea or feedback, maintaining moderate eye contact with your listeners shows that you are confident in your contributions. It says, "I believe in what I'm saying, and I'm here, present, with you in this conversation." Avoiding eye contact, on the other hand, can make you appear uncertain or disinterested, while too much eye contact might be perceived as confrontational.

If you struggle to make eye contact, here's one trick I use: wait to make eye contact until the last few words of your sentence; end with eye contact. You may be under the impression that you're supposed to maintain eye contact the entire time. Not true. In fact, prolonged eye contact may make you come across as either too intense or, heaven forbid, even kind of creepy. Instead, catch their eye at the end of your sentence. You won't lose any effectiveness.

Cadence, the rhythm and pace of your speech, also matters. An assertive cadence involves speaking clearly at a measured pace, allowing your words to be fully understood without rushing or hesitating. It's about giving each word its due, showing that you've thought about what you're saying and you mean it. For instance, when proposing a new strategy, speaking too quickly might suggest nervousness or a lack of confidence in your own idea, while speaking too slowly could be interpreted as uncertainty.

Together, a controlled tone, appropriate eye contact, and a deliberate cadence can significantly enhance the effectiveness of your communication. They make your assertiveness not only heard, but felt and seen. Whether you're asking for a promotion, setting a boundary, or simply expressing an opinion, how you present your message can be as impactful as the message itself. These elements, combined with clear, respectful language, define assertive communication and enable it to be a powerful tool for personal and professional growth.

I want you to quickly scan back over the ten lessons of this chapter. Pick the one that you wrestle with the most. Make that one lesson your focus for today, or tomorrow, or this week. Begin using those assertive words and phrases when the opportunity comes in the next conversation, the next text. See how it makes you feel. See how other people respond. And see how it makes you want to assert yourself more.

Using assertive words will build your confidence. And your growing confidence will cause you to speak more assertively more often. It's a positive feedback loop. So feed it. Once you feel good about using phrases from the lesson you picked out, start adding phrases from another lesson. Don't wait to find the right words to say two days later. Build your assertiveness vocabulary so that you know what to say now.

CHAPTER SUMMARY

- Confidence is a feeling, not a thing you can summon.
- You build confidence through being assertive; together, they create a positive feedback loop. The more assertive you are, the more confident you feel, and the more confident you feel, the more assertive you are.
- Word choice matters. Typically, the fewer words you use, the more confident you

sound. Eliminate unnecessary apologies and filler words to increase the strength of your sentences.

- When you unlock your assertive voice, you empower yourself to express your needs with confidence.

CHAPTER 8

Difficult People

Legal disputes between family members are the worst. Between friends is a close second.

The people you let into your life know a lot about you: what makes you happy and what makes you upset. When close relationships go south, they can be the nastiest sort of conflict, the type that brings out the absolute worst in a person. Sometimes the most difficult people in your life are either related to you or have a history with you, making the tough talks even tougher. Maybe you can relate.

I once had a case involving two middle-aged sisters. And it was about as fun as it sounds.

My client wanted to keep the business that the two had inherited operating and successful. The other sister wanted to sell the business and split the profits, on account of her having, let's just say, different life goals. They needed a clean break from what had become a constant source of conflict between them. The plan was for my client to buy out her sister's shares.

Despite multiple attempts to negotiate, my client's generosity and patience were continually met with stubbornness and, at times, outright hostility. The other sister insisted on painting my client as the antagonist of the story. When my client presented reasonable solutions, the other sister would find a way to twist her words and resort to hurtful comments and insults that went back as far as when they were kids. Things she knew would hurt.

"How long do I keeping playing nice?" my client asked me during a phone call.

"You always play nice," I said. "That doesn't mean you play soft. You don't need to push back. You just can't be pushed over."

Acknowledging that she'd tried everything to keep it peaceful and respect what her parents would want, my client had found her limit. Trying to "work it out" wasn't working. She needed a different strategy. Using the lessons you'll learn in this chapter, my client began standing up for herself in conversations with her sister. She started to find her voice.

The two agreed to meet in person (with attorneys) to try one last time to resolve their issues. My client was nervous walking in, but I could tell she had a new sense of confidence when she spoke. The discussion started off fine, but it wasn't long before the sister began ramping up the drama. At one point, she threw out something that was more than a comment. It was a grenade:

"And I've never liked you. You're dead to me anyway."

My client went silent. I knew from our many conversations that her sister's words cut like a knife. After using a long pause, she finally spoke.

"I need you to repeat that."

Her sister looked uncertain. She wasn't expecting that response. She looked as though she was about to say it again, but she couldn't.

"I'm—I'm not repeating that," she said, almost shaken.

"Then I won't be repeating this," my client said firmly. "I'm getting off this roller coaster. If you want to get off with me, do it now. And I've always loved you."

The sister teared up and asked for some time to speak to her attorney alone. A few minutes later, the case settled.

You've heard the advice that in difficult moments like these you need to be empathetic and try to reach common ground. I think that's right and it's noble. But sometimes, it's not practical. What do you do when you feel like your compassion has been exhausted? How do you communicate when you believe your empathy is being exploited or taken advantage of?

When Push Comes to Shove

Kindness alone doesn't always work. No amount of patience or gentle explanation makes a difference.

The person is committed to misunderstanding you. When it happens, you'll be tempted to do one of two things. You'll walk on eggshells, constantly adjusting your words and actions to avoid conflict altogether at the expense of your own authenticity and peace of mind. Or you'll double down, matching their negative energy tit-for-tat and round for round.

I want you to do neither. There's a third option. It involves using your new assertive voice to create responses that leave no room for misinterpretation, responses that have all the boldness of aggression with none of the disrespect.

There comes a point when it's time to stand up for yourself, when push comes to shove and you need to voice your disapproval. Yes, you're still going to show integrity. Yes, you're still going to show respect. But your response should be about showing that you respect yourself enough to speak up and say what is unacceptable to you.

The first thing to know about standing up for yourself is when to do it, because not everyone is worth getting out of your chair for. It's a know-your-worth mentality. Not everyone is worth your peace of mind. You have to know and consciously decide if the person standing in front of you is one who means something to you.

To assertively disagree and stand up for yourself is both an art and a skill. Here are the advanced tools you'll need the next time someone goes too far.

How to Deflect Insults, Belittling, and Rudeness

When you hear someone say something rude or insulting, understand that they're wanting something from you. That something is dopamine, the "feel-good hormone" that motivates and rewards you. Their search for dopamine has little to do with you personally. It's often a reflection of their own insecurities. Belittling others can make the powerless feel powerful, the ignored feel seen, and the jealous feel like they've gained something. They get dopamine from the attention of the spotlight or from their sense of control over your negative reaction.

It also distracts them from their own vulnerabilities by allowing them to focus on perceived or projected weaknesses in you, in the same way you may catch yourself judging someone. The other person feels less insecure, even if momentarily, knowing that they can give you insecurities too. They'll feel less upset knowing that you're upset. It's a cycle in which their temporary high comes at the cost of your confidence.

The key is to see these types of comments for what they truly are: an attempt to elicit a response.

Remember, it's not about you. It's about their need for your response.

So when they say something for their hit of dopamine, the worst thing you can do is give it to them. That's why you're not going to.

When they insult or offend you

"You're an idiot."
"You're a loser."
"You're ugly."

Whether it's name-calling or personal attacks on your character, looks, ability, or identity, these comments are meant to hurt. They might be aimed at your age, race, gender, or background. They're meant to cut deep, and they often hurt more because they're direct.

I know that when you get an insult it feels better to throw it right back. "Oh, I'm an idiot? Well, **you're** . . ." But that only ratchets up the problem. Maybe you can convince yourself that you're okay with that, but now **you're** the one wanting dopamine. The blows will continue to get thrown until one of you bows out and receives a momentary "win."

It's not worth it. Your value is too high for such low behavior.

When someone insults or offends you, try these steps:

1. Give it a long pause

The long pause gives their words a chance to echo back to them. The pause also allows their words to fall before they get to you, as I'll discuss in chapter eleven, which keeps you from getting defensive.

A long pause makes them rethink their words and question whether they will stand by them or take them back. Remember, the awkward pause will make them squirm, and that's okay. And most of all, the silence **takes away their dopamine.**

2. Slowly repeat what they said

Often, the silence is all you need to say. If it requires more, repeat what they said back to them very . . . slowly. Here, you're the echo. You're ensuring that they heard every word of what they said.

3. Keep breathing out

When you repeat their words back, it will either clear up the confusion or add fuel to the fire. Go to your breath. In that moment, you need to rely on breath control to make sure you don't tighten your body or muddle your thinking. If you enter into a state of shallow breathing, there's a higher risk that you'll have a delayed display of emotion or anger and lose the high ground. If needed, assert a boundary, as you'll learn in the next chapter.

When they belittle, patronize, or condescend to you

> "Let me put this in terms that you'll understand."
> "Oh wow, you finally lost some weight. Good for you."
> "It's cute how you thought you did it right."

These comments are meant to diminish your efforts, intelligence, or status. It's the idea that they're "talking down" to you and explaining what you already know. Unlike more aggravated insults, these remarks are often indirect. There is typically a sense of feigned or pretend praise, or friendliness, that's underscored with a put-down to reduce your significance.

When someone belittles, patronizes, or condescends to you, try these steps:

1. Make them say it again

Ask them to repeat it. That's it. When you ask the other person to repeat what they just said, you take all the fun—a.k.a. dopamine—out of it. It's like throwing a wet, soggy blanket over their words. They're also not expecting that reply. When someone makes a belittling remark, they expect the spotlight to turn to you. But when you ask them to repeat what they just said, the spotlight jerks right back to them. They'll become uncomfortable. The result is often a quick reply of "Never mind," or "Uh, I meant . . ." as they try to readjust their response. It can be as simple as:

- "I need you to repeat that."
- "I need you to say that again."
- "I didn't get all of that—can you repeat it?"

2. Ask a question of outcome

Regardless of whether they have the guts to repeat the comment, you're going to respond using a question of outcome. This type of question seeks to highlight and project the reaction that they tried to elicit. Again, you're verbalizing the echo of them they need to hear.

- "Did you want that to hurt?"
- "Did you want that to embarrass me?"
- "Was that supposed to make me feel small?"
- "Did that feel good to say out loud?"

3. Reply with silence

No matter their answer, let your silence be your reply. It's better not to respond. Most likely, they'll have a terrible excuse or say they're just joking or start fumbling over their words and backtracking. Let their poor behavior linger as your silence shows you to be the one with control and composure.

When they're rude or dismissive

"Oh, you're still talking?"
"No one asked you."
"I feel dumber just by listening to you."

These comments are the more common, general remarks that go against social norms and show a lack of respect. They can be direct or indirect, and they're abrasive. The goal of these comments is to invalidate your thoughts or beliefs.

When someone is rude to you or dismissive of your views, try these steps:

1. Give it a short pause

Pause just long enough to consider their words. Here, you're using silence as a scale, weighing their words to decide if what they said is worth your time and effort.

2. Ask a question of intent

These questions are similar to outcome-based questions but instead are input-focused, seeking to highlight the sound of their words and probing into their intentions. Questions like:

- "Did you mean for that to sound rude?" (or offensive or dismissive)
- "Did you mean for that to come across short?"
- "What did you intend with that statement?"
- "How did you expect me to react to that?"
- "Was that meant to be helpful, or hurtful?"

3. Wait

The vast majority of the time, the other person will clarify or apologize and readjust their comment with something like "Oh goodness, no, not at all, what I meant was . . ." If this happens, congratulations, you avoided taking things personally and potentially throwing a wrench in a relationship.

If, however, their intent was ill-willed, leave it. Give them silence and move on.

This formula doesn't just work for verbal conversation. It works for written communication too. A quick email or text with "Did you mean for that to sound short?" can cure most poorly worded and shortsighted messages.

Pushing Back Against Bad Apologies

They know they messed up. You know they messed up. And still they avoid the honest apology.

Getting someone to apologize for something they did to hurt you can be downright miserable and can make it hurt even more, like salt in the wound. When someone withholds an apology, it can feel like a denial of your feelings, of your experience. It deepens the rift, as the lack of a real apology leaves your hurt unacknowledged and the issue pushed further away from reconciliation. As the healing process is delayed, trust and respect begin to fall.

There is no difference between refusing to offer an apology and dressing up an excuse to sound like one. If anything, dressing up an excuse is even worse, because the other person knows exactly what you need but chooses to withhold it. They know they should. They know they could. But they won't. It goes back to the fear of being wrong. Admitting fault or blame can be a blow to the ego. It makes you confront your own shortcomings. To own up to a mistake and apologize is difficult for many people.

And you've been there too. Times when you didn't feel like saying you're sorry—"I'm **not** sorry, I've done **nothing** wrong." Understand that if you value the other person in your life, and that person is truly hurt, withholding an apology is corrosive. And what does it cost you? Really? What does an apology cost you, even if you don't fully agree with it?

I'm not talking about the people who play the victim to manipulate you and make you apologize. There are other strategies for dealing with that. I'm talking about everyday, you-hurt-my-feelings conversations. It's okay to say, "I'm not ready to apologize at the moment. I'm too upset and I need to calm down first." That's communication. That's real. But to withhold an apology because you don't believe someone deserves it is to play both judge and jury.

No one can tell you how to feel or what to feel.

It's like someone punching you in the arm and telling you it didn't hurt. They don't get to decide that. And while there's nothing you can do to force someone to apologize, you can stand up for yourself and let it be known that you will no longer be accepting bad, useless apologies.

Bad apologies come in all shapes and sizes, but some are more common than others. The following are the ones you're most likely to hear and have absolutely heard before:

The no-empathy apology

This sounds like: "Well, I'm sorry that you feel that way."

Your response: "Don't apologize for my feelings, apologize for what you did."

This apology sidesteps all accountability. Rather than addressing their misconduct, they shift the focus to your reaction. This response re-centers the conversation to where it belongs: the other person's actions. You're sending the message of **No, these are my feelings, I got those. I'll be accountable for those. You be accountable for you.** You're highlighting the fact that someone being sorry for how you feel isn't an apology for what they've done. It is not their place to be sorry about how you feel. It's their place to be sorry about the behavior that caused those feelings.

The no-apology apology

This sounds like: "I'm sorry if I did something wrong," or "I'm sorry if I upset you."

Your response: "I need you to change the **if** to **that**."

By inserting **if** into the apology, the other person makes the apology seem conditional and uncertain, as if what they did is still up for debate. Your response instructs them to remove the conditional language. By asking the other person to change **if** to **that**, you're guiding them toward owning their actions more directly. This shifts the apology from a hypothetical to an acknowledgment of actual harm. "I'm sorry **that** I upset you" is more sincere and meaningful.

The excuse apology

This sounds like: "I'm sorry, okay? I've just been so stressed lately."

Your response: "You don't need to apologize for your stress. I need you to apologize for your words."

This apology deflects responsibility for their behavior to their external environment, like work, or the kids, or stress. But understand that those are all things that have happened to **them**. They haven't happened to you. And you shouldn't pay the price for them.

This response takes away the power of their excuse. Their stress didn't say something hurtful. Their work didn't make you upset. Redirect the responsibility back to whom it belongs.

The toxic apology

This sounds like: "I'm sorry that I'm such a horrible person," or "I'm sorry that you're so perfect."

Your response: "I'm willing to accept an apology."

This apology isn't just toxic. It's manipulative. And they're hoping that you'll take the bait. Here's what they're hoping it looks like:

YOUR MOM: "I'm sorry that I'm such a bad mother."

YOU: "You're not a bad mother, you just need to understand that . . ."

YOUR MOM: "Yes I am, I'm horrible. That's what you think. You always try to . . ."

And off they go, far, far away from the hurt that they caused you. These kinds of apologies frame the other person as the victim in an attempt to garner sympathy and make you the comforter. This response keeps you out of the trap. It's neutral and measured, and it asserts what you're willing to accept and what you're not willing to entertain. If they try again, simply repeat it: "I'm willing to accept an apology."

The justification apology

This sounds like: "I was just kidding," "I was just joking," or "I was just messing around."

Your response: "Then be funnier," or "Then find new material," or "I wasn't."

This kind of apology is a veiled attempt to minimize the impact of their actions and suggests that what they did shouldn't have been taken seriously. It undermines the validity of your feelings and implies that the problem is with you—your lack of a sense of humor, your sensitivity, your overreaction. This response counters that tactic and makes clear that humor never justifies harm.

The End of Interruptions

Not all interruptions are bad. Maybe the other person is excited. Maybe they can't help it. Interruptions are common and expected in laid-back conversations with friends and in casual settings. That's not an issue. But when you're trying to have a serious conversation, a heart-to-heart, or a business meeting with company-wide ramifications, interruptions can be infuriating.

Here's how to put a stop to them.

Step 1: Let the other person interrupt you

The first time they interrupt, let them.

Yes, let them.

But just the first time.

Allowing the other person to interrupt you on the first swing serves two purposes.

1. Their interruption gives you the high ground as the more mature, more reasonable person. The less impulsive, the more thoughtful. If you cut them off too soon with "Uh, **excuse me**, I was still talking," it can come across as too harsh, often making you

look unforgiving or insecure. Remember, confident people know how to select their timing. The other person hasn't taken anything away from you. If anything, their interruption makes them look bad. Don't steal their negative light and put it on yourself.

2. Their interruption lets them get their impulsive thoughts out. It's at this stage that what the other person says is primarily emotion-driven. It's a knee-jerk reaction. If they have to speak their mind so badly that they have to say it right at that moment, they weren't going to listen to what you were about to say anyway. You can't pour water into a glass that's already full. So let them spill it out.

As soon as they're finished with their thought, go back to exactly where you left off. Don't address their comment. Don't get carried away on a tangent. Restart your sentence. This signals to the other person that you weren't done talking without risking your credibility and that you're committed to communicating in complete messages.

Step 2: Use their name

Say their name to stop their interruption. Names catch people's attention. If you cut the other person off with "Hey!" or "Just listen!" they'll get more defensive and closed off. But if you say their name, even if it's forceful or stern, they tend to remain open.

Using their name is also a good way to stop someone who is dominating a conversation or talking over people. Say their name out loud at a normal level. If it doesn't stop them, repeat it while increasing your volume.

Step 3: Correct the behavior

Here, you're going to assert yourself with statements that are **I** driven rather than **you** driven (think "You're interrupting me" or "Don't interrupt me!"). Use one of these responses in a calm, collected manner:

- "I cannot hear you when you interrupt me."
- "I will listen to you when I'm finished."
- "I want to listen to you. I need to finish my thought before I do."

These responses work because they not only are direct but also position you in a way that the other person has to expose themself in order to oppose you. Interrupting again would place their poor behavior too far out on a ledge as a blatant violation. It would mean they're not interested in being heard, which means they're not truly interested in conversation but rather in wanting to hear themself speak. Most people aren't willing to look that bad.

More often than not, after you follow these steps, they won't interrupt you in the conversation again. By allowing them to interrupt the first time, calmly using their name, and holding your ground, you've created a power dynamic in your favor while still maintaining your credibility.

Here's what that could look like between you and a coworker, Alex:

YOU: "The main issue with the current project timeline is that—"

ALEX: "Listen, we've always made it work, okay? Timeline or no timeline. I mean, if it were up to me, we'd already have this moving forward without needing input from management . . ."

You say nothing and allow Alex to finish, using breath control to maintain steady composure.

ALEX: ". . . And I understand that you and I don't always see eye to eye, but I know that what I bring to the table provides value."

YOU: "The main issue with the current project timeline is that it doesn't account for the new budget approvals, which may slow down the—"

ALEX: "It won't. I've seen this before, okay? There's this—"

YOU: "Alex."

Alex pauses.

YOU: "I can't hear you when you interrupt me. Let me finish."

Alex nods and acknowledges your turn to speak.

This method keeps the relationship respectful. Imagine instead that at the first interruption, you angrily say, "I'm talking!" You'll lose the power dynamic, as now you're the one who appears more emotional and needy. Other sarcastic phrases like "Did the middle of my sentence interrupt the beginning of yours?" may seem cool, but they only lose you respect and make you less desirable to listen to. Using your assertive voice to stop interruptions maintains respect through measured responses.

A Better Way to Disagree

One of the important uses of your assertive language is to voice disagreement. It's part of standing up for yourself. But what you say and how you say it when you disagree can be all the difference between sounding assertive and sounding insecure. It's easy to disagree poorly (think "Nuh-uh!" or "Not true!"). It's much harder to disagree effectively.

Handling disagreement goes back to a core theme

of this book: winning an argument often loses you more. You can disagree with another's viewpoint without trying to win or play a trump card. Voicing disagreement is standing up for yourself. Pushing your disagreement at the expense of another's voice, however, is standing over someone else.

Here are some advanced techniques that will improve your ability to voice disagreement without losing ground—or taking it. The next time you need to disagree, try this.

Apply the Is it worth it? filter

Sometimes, it feels as though the other person is looking for an argument. Like they're trying to suck you into a vortex, where everything and anything you say is twisted and turned or boomeranged back to make you agree with them. Maybe it's about politics. Maybe it's about religion. Maybe it's about how the towels should be folded (actually, never mind the last one). The point is, don't let them put you in that position where you feel like your back is against the wall or like you're hitting your head against one.

Before it goes too far, apply a quick **Is it worth it?** filter. Ask, "Is this something we have to agree on?"

For example:

YOUR PARTNER: "I'm thinking about changing up the laundry detergent to this brand I saw a commercial for on TV. What do you think?"

YOU: "I'd rather not. I like the one we've been using."

YOUR PARTNER: "But the other one is also supposed to be more eco-friendly. It's better for the environment."

YOU: "I get that, I'm just not convinced it'll work as well as the one we have."

YOUR PARTNER: "Why is it that you never want to go along with something unless it's your idea?"

YOU: "Is this something we have to agree on?"

YOUR PARTNER: "No, I guess you're right."

Immediately, this question forces the other person to evaluate the priority of the conversation. This technique is especially good for what 99 percent of arguments are about—nothing. Use this **Is it worth it?** filter if you find yourself in disagreement over mundane issues or arguments about things that may never come to pass.

Sure, they may want you to agree with them. But do you have to? Usually, the answer is no.

If somehow the answer is yes, move to the next filter: **Is this something we have to agree on** now? For example:

YOU: "Is this something we have to agree on?"

YOUR PARTNER: "I mean, yeah, I think we should."

YOU: "Is this something we have to agree on right at this moment?"

YOUR PARTNER: "Oh, no, I suppose not. We can try it out first and then decide."

This question forces the other person to evaluate the timing of the conversation. It's common in close relationships to argue about things that'll never happen. You're arguing on what-ifs and what-abouts. By asking if an immediate agreement is necessary, you introduce the possibility of postponing the decision until more information is available or until both of you are more ready to address it. Asking to postpone is a quick way to defuse disagreement by grounding the conversation on what really matters in the moment.

Use your vantage point

When you respond with "I disagree," it's direct. And in many contexts, it's too direct. "I disagree" can expose you to a volley of back-and-forth arguments, potentially escalating the situation unnecessarily. That's because while you say, "I disagree," the other person hears, "You're wrong." And that can light up their psychological triggers of social evaluation or competence.

Now, there are times when they really are wrong, like if they're trying to convince you that the sky is green. That's not what I'm talking about. I'm making the point that "I disagree," while direct (which is good), can create more problems for you because it can make the other person feel shot down and defensive (not good). Even if you say, "I **respectfully** disagree," there's nothing respectful about it—and they know that because they can feel it.

Instead, opt for phrases that signal viewpoints, not verdicts. That is, convey your opinion from a particular vantage point as opposed to a blunt dismissal. This strategy opens up space for dialogue rather than confrontation. To use your vantage point effectively, try one of these three phrases:

1. "I see things differently."

When you frame your response as a difference in viewpoint, it's like telling someone what you see from where you're sitting in a room. It widens the perspectives on the subject like a lens zooming out of magnification. Notice the difference between "You're wrong" and "From where I'm sitting, I see something different." The idea of seeing something differently makes your response about sharing perceptions instead of disputing facts. This response is useful for situations when:

- They're trying to press a one-size-fits-all solution
- You need to introduce a nuanced perspective or add context
- They overlook aspects that you give higher or lower importance

2. "I take another approach."

This response indicates that while the approach is different, the goal is the same. You get the same result, but you just have a different method of showing your work. There are direct routes, and there are scenic routes. Each has its benefits. Each gets you to where you want to be. The benefit of this response is that it focuses both of your sights on the ultimate goal. It emphasizes collaboration over conflict. You both want the best for whatever it is, such as your family, the company, or your country. You just take another approach to it. This response is effective in situations when:

- You disagree about what's "best" for a common objective
- Their method or plan of action lacks consideration of other factors
- They're fixated on doing things a certain way

3. "I tend to lean the opposite."

By using history and experience as a backstop, you give yourself an anchoring point or foundation to express your view. Instead of challenging the other person, such as when you say, "I don't agree with you," this response relies upon a history of what you typically do, what you prefer to do, or how you tend to think. Arguing from a method of preference keeps your position from getting confrontational. You're stating what you normally do, and people are more willing to accept that than a quick reaction that slams a door in their face. This response is helpful in situations when:

- Their position conflicts with your values
- You need to express experience over the subject matter
- You see a different conclusion from the shared evidence

Knowing the right way to disagree positions you as the calmer, more controlled person in the room. Phrases like the preceding ones help continue conversations rather than cutting them off. But what if someone is insistent and pushes back again? Simply repeat the phrase as many times as you need. The other person will get the point: you're not one to be pushed over.

When confronted by a difficult person, you don't have to play their game. Refuse to let bad apologies, repeated interruptions, and bids for disagreement disrupt your confidence. When you stand firm, speak with an assertive voice, and deny the other person the dopamine they're seeking, you'll gain and maintain the high ground.

CHAPTER SUMMARY

- Standing your ground and speaking up for yourself is self-care.
- The key to responding to hurtful or offensive comments is to refuse to give in to their search for dopamine.
- Prevent the immediate reward of a dopamine spike by using strategies that delay your answer, like taking a long pause, slowly repeating their words back to them, or using a question of intent.
- Be firm against bad apologies, interruptions, and bids for disagreement by calling out the behavior and using concise, assertive phrases.
- When you refuse to play down to someone else's poor communication habits, you keep the high ground and maintain credibility.

CHAPTER 9

Boundaries

You don't need a relatable story for this one. Saying no is hard.

You didn't have a problem saying no when you were young. But somewhere along the way as you grew older, you found out that saying no had a cost. Saying no to peer pressure made you feel left out. Saying no to your parents or a teacher meant punishment or discipline. Saying no to certain activities made you feel like something was wrong with you or that you wouldn't be liked.

So you acquiesced, you compromised, you people-pleased for the sake of everyone else's peace except your own. You prioritized others' comfort and desires over your own well-being, often at the expense of what you really wanted. Over time, it turned into a pattern: overcommit, stress, resent, and repeat.

Learning to say no is not only reclaiming your power to make decisions that honor your needs but also rediscovering the childlike freedom to choose without fear.

You **can** relearn that it's okay to prioritize your well-being, to say what you need to say in a way that honors you and the world around you. And when you do, you'll find that it'll make you healthier, happier, and more authentic to who you truly are.

Let's start small. I got you.

Ding!

In the corner of your laptop screen you see a notification for a message from a coworker.

"Hey! Wanna grab coffee tomorrow at that new café? Need my caffeine fix lol"

Ugh.

Without hesitation, your gut wants to say no. It's not that you don't like this person. They're nice enough, really. But you see them as a work friend, not a **friend** friend. Really more of a repeat acquaintance. And you don't necessarily feel like giving up an hour making small talk when you already have so much going on.

You're faced with three choices:

A. Accept it
B. Decline it
C. Ignore it

You and I both know good and well that you want to choose C. In fact, I bet you've already ignored the message and minimized the window.

Yes, ignoring it works, but for all the wrong reasons. You have a limited number of ignores until the other person catches on that you're avoiding them. When you hit that limit, the other person will fill in their own blank as to why you're avoiding them, and it's almost guaranteed to be worse than the truth of why you want to say no. It's also a cop-out. Sure, you could wait until tomorrow when you see your coworker at the office, or send a reply, "Oh, sorry! I totally missed this! Darn. Would've loved to." Come on. How many times can you do that? How does that show respect to your coworker or to yourself?

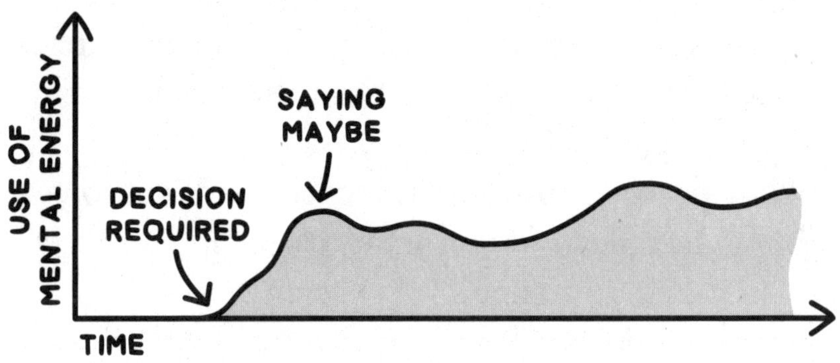

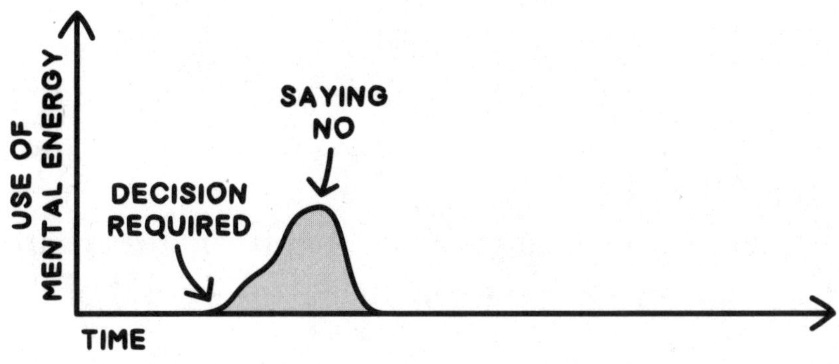

Here's another reason why ignoring isn't the move: the decision is still taking up mental space, living in your head rent-free. Every time you see that unread message, every time the thought crosses your mind, there's the weight (no matter how negligible) of an unresolved issue. Ignoring it doesn't make it go away. It only prolongs the decision and ensures a secondary conversation down the road. The coworker will ask for another time you're available, putting you on the spot again. More wasted time, more wasted stress.

When you get an invitation that you don't want to accept, whether it's for a dinner party with that couple you're not crazy about, a night out when you want to stay in, or that getaway that doesn't interest you, you're not negotiating with the other person.

You're negotiating with yourself.

Your peace of mind isn't negotiable. Even to you. Confidence means if you want to accept, you accept. If you don't, you don't.

How would you say no to your coworker's message? I'm assuming you're thinking of something like this:

"Hey! Thanks for the invite, but I can't. I'm just super busy right now. Sorry!"

How good do you feel about responses like this one? Do they feel genuine? Do they feel comfortable? Likely not.

Here's how you're going to fix it. If you read chapter seven, you know to go ahead and get rid of the unnecessary apology and involuntary justification. After that, you're left with this:

"Thanks for the invite, but I can't. ~~I'm just super busy right now. Sorry!~~"

Broken down, there are two elements. There's **gratitude** (thanks for inviting me) followed by the **no** (but I can't). The problem with this sequence of beginning with gratitude and ending with no is that it's too tempting to tag on a justification or an excuse to the end of the sentence. For example, "Thanks for the invite, but I can't . . . **because** I have this thing I need to go to and I'm too busy and . . ."

Another problem is that this sequence tees the other person up to ask you why or inquire further, because when you end with "but I can't," they almost feel like you're expecting them to show concern and respond, "Oh bummer, why not?" or "How come?" And one of the biggest problems with this order is that it causes you to use the word **but**, as in, "Thank you, **but** . . ." The **but** takes away from your previous statement of gratitude.

There's a better way. To start building your confidence through saying no to simple invitations and social offers, try these three steps:

Step 1: Say no.

- "I can't."
- "I won't be able to."

- "I need to say no / I need to take a pass."
- "I made a promise to myself that . . ."

Step 2: Show gratitude.

- "Thank you for inviting me / including me / thinking of me."
- "That's so kind of you / that means a lot."
- "I appreciate you asking me."
- "I'm flattered / honored."

Step 3: Show kindness.

- "Sounds like a wonderful time!"
- "Hope it goes well! / I know it will be great!"
- "I've heard good things about . . ."
- "Hope you're doing well!"

This sequence works for several reasons.

First, you begin with the no because it's direct, and direct is kind.

Second, you layer the no with gratitude, which acknowledges the value of the gesture and also reciprocates thoughtfulness. By saying no and **then** using gratitude, you remove the need to use **but** in your response.

Lastly, ending with a statement of kindness finishes the response on a more pleasant note, one that doesn't draw a "Why not?" but instead encourages a "You're welcome!" or "You'll be missed!" And especially in text or written communication, feel free to use emojis when appropriate to help give the reader emotional context.

So get out your imaginary laptop again and look at the invite for coffee with your coworker. Rather than removing the notification or not responding, you reply:

> "I can't. Thank you for the invite. I've heard good things about it!"

Rarely will a clean, confident reply like that ever draw an objection or pushback. Compare that reply to the more awkward "Thanks for the invite, but I can't make it."

A stern warning: If you're still asked for a justification, an explanation, or a reason why you said no—do not give in to it. Unless the other person is someone you love and trust and feel comfortable being 100 percent open with, don't give in to it. If you feel the need to reply, simply repeat the turndown. In the coffee scenario, if your coworker messaged back, "Aw why not?" you'd reply by repeating your turndown: "I can't." At that point, it's colder for a reason. And that reason is you don't need to excuse or justify why you're choosing what's right for you.

No **is** the only reason you need. No is a complete sentence.

Embrace the feelings of disappointment. Work

through them. Be okay with them. Don't let go of your confidence. This is part of the process of reclaiming your needs and finding your freedom. Understand that when you feel like you're disappointing the other person, it's typically 98 percent ego and 2 percent truth. That is, part of your feelings of disappointment is really you convincing yourself that your presence is so needed that the other person will be crushed if you say no. That you're so vital to their good time that the other person isn't emotionally resilient enough to handle it.

Rarely are you or I that important. Take a big breath and move forward. When it comes to standing up for yourself, disappointing someone often means you're doing something right.

But what about the harder conversations, like the comments and questions that make you uncomfortable? The ones that come from people you know to be toxic or manipulative? The ones that ask too much of you?

How do you say no then?

How to Build a Boundary

You've probably heard of a boundary as it relates to self-respect or self-esteem. And though you may be familiar with the topic, having the words to effectively create a boundary requires a particular skill. It's about more than setting limits. It's how to communicate those limits assertively. Whereas saying no to a social invitation may be simply closing a door, asserting a boundary is more like building a fortress with a moat.

Defining the perimeter

Typically, you'll hear people refer to personal boundaries as "drawing a line" or "crossing a line." That's a half-baked description. A boundary isn't a line. It's a perimeter. Think of a circle or a rectangle: there's no end and no beginning. The area is fully enclosed, creating a defined space that is distinct and unique to its owner. When you drive around a neighborhood or even a country road, it's common to see a fence. That fence is important. It tells you that the property belongs to someone, that someone values what's on the other side. The fence is both a force to keep people out and a warning of how close they can get until they're trespassing, visually communicating the limits of the space. Personal boundaries work much the same way.

It begins with what's important to you. Your boundaries inform the outside world of your values, what you value deep down. Maybe it's your health, your family, your career, your well-being, your self-respect. These are the things in your life worth protecting.

For example, let's say your family is your top priority. That's not a boundary, it's a **value**. And you let the world outside know it's your value when you say no to that networking event that would've meant you'd miss good-night prayers and tuck-ins. Or when you pass on that job offer that would've meant more time away from your partner. Just like that fence, it's a bright-line indication of where your border sits.

Maybe your priority is your mental health. When you say no to that family reunion that always makes you feel bad about yourself, or part ways with that friend who is always a "taker" who drains your emotional energy, other people take notice of the "fence" you're building.

Your actions and choices define the boundary around the things you value. It's your actions and choices that inform others of what matters to you. The importance of your family or the value of your mental health doesn't turn into a boundary until you begin making intentional choices that put others on notice that **they are not allowed in.** Part of building your confidence is being the bouncer to your own self-esteem. You have to let others know what's allowed and what isn't.

The benefits of boundaries are innumerable. They're your cornerstone for healthy relationships, honest communication, and self-respect. By building boundaries, you not only protect your emotional and mental well-being but also educate others to understand and respect your needs and limits. Boundaries also help you prevent burnout and resentment by making sure you're not overextended, allowing you to allocate your time and energy to what truly matters. They enable you to make choices aligned with your values and priorities, promoting your freedom and autonomy. Boundaries are also a form of self-care: you're showing up for yourself enough to protect your peace. As you become more comfortable creating these boundaries, you'll notice a deeper sense of control over your life and an enhanced ability to navigate interactions with assertiveness, building your confidence.

Knowing your manual

I want you to go back in your mind and recall a time someone spoke to you in a way that made you feel small. A fight with an ex. An argument with a superior. A time when you felt pushed around or less yourself, without any boundary to help you.

Remember specifically how you felt. If I had to guess, you didn't feel an overwhelming sense of control. You felt cornered, powerless, constantly in a state of reacting to the threat in front of you. As if your sense of autonomy were taken away, much like someone holding the remote control to your emotions, pushing your buttons, flipping through channels without your consent and leaving you to watch your pain play out.

Instead of handing over the remote control to your emotions, allowing others to push your buttons and hold all the control, get into the mindset of giving out manuals. A list of automatic nos. These manuals give voice to your boundaries, instructing the other person in detail about how you operate. Think of it like explaining the rules of a new card game. You're providing the rules and instructions by which things will move forward. Here's what the difference sounds like:

- When they have the remote control, you shout: "Stop yelling at me!"

- When you give a manual, you say: "I don't respond to that volume."

- When they have the remote control, you yell: "You can't speak to me that way!"

- When you give a manual, you say: "I don't accept the way you're speaking to me."

One says, **I have no control**. The other states, **I am in control.**

The manual isn't just for them, either. It's for you too. And that raises a good question: Do you know what your manual says? There's a possibility you may not. If **you** don't, how will anyone else? The solution is to make a numbered list, a set of instructions, of how—in your very next conversation—you will engage in communication. Write them down in full sentences, laying out your operator's manual. You need to know for yourself what you will say no to and what you won't allow past your boundary. For example:

- "I don't respond to disrespect."
- "I will not allow others to tell me or decide how I feel."
- "I don't engage in conversation when I'm not ready."
- "I don't dismiss my intuition as irrelevant."
- "I won't compromise my peace for the sake of appeasement."
- "I don't participate in gossip or character assassination."

You'll find that the act of writing them down gives you a sense of assuredness. By following your manual, you'll feel more confident in standing your ground the next time someone insults you, stonewalls you, or puts words in your mouth. The next time someone says, "You don't even care about my opinion, you only care about yourself," you'll feel empowered enough to calmly respond, "I get to decide that." You're replacing the other person's ability to influence your emotions with a process that works for your good.

Enforcing the boundary

Once you know the value you need to protect and you know your manual, it's time to enforce the boundary. That means speaking up and telling the other person what they've run into, and most important, telling them that they won't be going any further. Here's how to assert your boundary.

1. Begin with the boundary

Begin with an "I" statement like you learned in chapter eight, then insert your boundary. Using **I** makes it clear that this is your boundary, your choice. If you've done your homework, this part should be the easiest. Depending on your value, it could sound like:

- I don't accept how you're treating me.
- I don't work on weekends.
- I don't drink alcohol.

Keep in mind, boundaries don't always have to be **I don't**. They can also redirect conversations, reset focus, and clarify your interest in constructive communication. Here's a good rule of thumb:

- **Tell them why you're there.** When they bring up an unrelated issue or try to distract, re-center the conversation. This is a boundary of presence.
  - **"I'm here because you matter to me."**

- **Tell them what you're there to talk about.** If they raise past issues or attack your character, correct the focus. This is a boundary of purpose.
  - **"I'm here to talk about what you said to me last Friday."**

- **Tell them where you're not going.** When they say something outlandish or attempt to get an emotional reaction, be firm. This is a boundary of integrity.
  - **"I'm not going there with you."**

Once you assert your boundary, it's a full stop. Don't be tempted to justify or explain. You've now set it on their side of the court to decide if they're going to respect your boundary or not.

2. Add the consequence

If the other person has made it clear that they do not intend to respect your boundary, add a consequence. This is what will happen if they continue to cross your boundary. There are two steps to it.

- The first is conditional: "If you continue to . . ."

- The second is the action step: "I'm going to . . ." As you'll recall from chapter seven, this phrase creates confidence, but this time it supports enforcing your boundary.

Here's what the boundary looks like after adding on a consequence:

- "I don't accept how you're treating me. **If you continue to treat me this way, I'm going to end the conversation."**

- "I don't work on weekends. **If you continue to schedule me on weekends, I'm going to find a place that supports my commitment to family."**

- "I don't drink alcohol. **If you continue to pressure me about it, I'm going to leave."**

3. Follow through

This part is the most difficult. If you're going to give a consequence, you have to mean it. Asserting yourself is telling the other person what you're going to do, then doing it. That means if they continue to ignore your boundary, you'll walk away from the conversation. You'll start looking for another job. You'll leave the party and lean on friends who respect your choices. You are showing that you say what you mean and mean what you say. You can't take one single step back. Whatever emotional response comes out of their mouth, you can't let that bait you into a conversation that erases the boundary you just set. Consistency is crucial.

How Setting Boundaries Changes Your Relationships

Once you begin creating and enforcing boundaries, there's something you need to know. Not everyone will like it. Some will even hate it. But they'll still respect you for it.

Boundaries have a way of sifting out those who are with you not because of who you are but rather because of what they need you to be. Even close friends. Even family members. There will be people who prefer the version of you without boundaries. This is a time for watching and observing who is in your corner, who your real people are. The ones who love you will support you. The ones who love you for only what you give to them will be against you. People who criticize your boundaries are simply reacting to a loss of privilege. It's almost as if whereas they were previously able to cut in line, now they have to wait like everyone else.

Their discomfort over your boundary is not a sign that it's wrong, it's a sign that it's working.

Embrace the thought of "No, **I don't have to** make this make sense to you. My boundaries were not put up to make you feel comfortable. They were put up for me."

Some people won't understand right away, and that's okay. Give them the grace to settle with the change. It will be a time when relationships are tested and recalibrated.

A quick note: You don't want to be the person who has too many boundaries, either. The type who has so many that it abuses your responsibilities, like not agreeing to basic collaboration or reasonable requests. A boundary isn't a catchall excuse. It doesn't justify bad behavior. It doesn't relieve you of your obligations. Too many boundaries can be counterproductive. Stick to setting a perimeter around the things you truly value in your life.

Boundaries are the bouncer for your well-being. They reinforce what you'll allow in and prevent what you don't need from entering your life. So make sure your bouncer is bold and visible. Think about that one person coming to mind who you know you need to have **that** talk with. What boundaries do you need to put up? What consequences do you need to set? And how will you promise yourself that you'll follow through?

When you've spent time with these questions, you'll spend more time with the relationships that fill your cup instead of pouring it out.

CHAPTER SUMMARY

- No is a complete sentence.
- You get over the fear of saying no by learning to embrace the consequences. Become comfortable with disappointing people and trust that they are more emotionally resilient than you've made them in your mind.
- Your actions and choices define the boundary around the things you value. If you want to know what someone values, look for where the boundary sits.
- Give others an operator's manual for how to communicate with you—not a remote control. Inform them what you will and will not allow past your boundary.
- If your boundary creates discomfort for another person, it's not a sign that the boundary is wrong. It's a sign that it's working.

Rule 3:

Say It to Connect

CHAPTER 10

Frames

I remember the first time my momma took me back-to-school shopping for new tennis shoes. We walked into Parkdale Mall, past the food court, and rounded the corner, where I could see a large storefront that said Foot Locker in red neon lights. I was so excited. I had planned out in my mind the exact type of shoe I'd get. It needed to make me jump high, so of course it needed to give me lots of air. It also needed to make me run fast, so it couldn't be too bulky. And it had to look **cool**.

As we walked into the store, my mouth dropped. There were **tons** of shoes. They all looked like they could make me jump high and run fast. They all looked cool.

My poor momma. I about drove her and the patient store associate crazy trying on every different pair of shoes. Each time she'd mash her thumb down on my big toe to check the fit. (Does every mom do that?) Each time she'd make me walk to the end of the store and come back. There were so many choices. It was overwhelming. I took forever.

Well, eventually, she'd had enough of it. She walked over to the wall, grabbed two different pairs, turned back around to me, and said, "Choose one."

"Wha-what? What about all the other ones?" I asked.

"Nope," she said, shaking her head and giving me the look. "Choose."

I chose my first pair of Nike Shox, which happened to be the very first pair I tried on.

What my wise momma knew: fewer choices can lead to better outcomes.

Conversations are the same. If a conversation has no goal, it'll feel as though you're talking about nothing. If a conversation has too many goals, it'll still feel as though you're talking about nothing. And no, I'm not referring to casual conversations, the catch-up talks with your friends and coworkers, or the nightly review of your day with your partner. I'm talking about conversations that need to achieve a specific goal: to connect. When you limit the pathways the conversation can take, you're helping yourself and the other person by making it easier to connect and find each other in the conversation.

I can't promise that this strategy will make you run faster or jump higher.

But I can promise it works.

What Is a Conversational Frame?

To create a clear connection with someone, you need to set a frame around your conversations. As a picture frame sets borders and enhances artwork, a frame around a conversation limits off-topics and amplifies the attention to the subject of conversation.

Framing ensures that the other person has fewer choices in the conversation. It narrows the focus of the discussion. With a frame, there's no wondering why you're talking, what you're talking about, or how it's supposed to end. You tell them your needs as well as your expectations, creating a "same page" mindset. Like playing off the same sheet music. You both know the song, the notes, and the time signature.

You'll also make it clear that off-topic or irrelevant issues are out of frame. There's less temptation to veer off course because your frame establishes the playbook.

Without a perimeter, the argument wanders around and can't settle on a topic—like looking for the perfect pair of new shoes on a wall. The argument's subject moves from place to place, retraces its steps, or goes far, far away from where the conversation started. That's why you can begin an argument talking about one thing and end it talking about something completely different. If your subject gets loose, your frame is the herd dog.

When a discussion happens without a frame, any number of unhelpful results can happen:

- The conversation lasts longer because the subject is unlimited.
- The longer you talk, the more susceptible your words are to misinterpretation, confusion, and misunderstanding.
- You leave the conversation feeling like nothing moved forward, or worse, like it moved two steps backward.

Conversations without a direction are sure to get lost. Vague conversation openings like "Hey, can we talk? So anyway, remember a few months ago when . . ." or "I need to tell you something. It's probably nothing, but . . ." aren't helpful—and can even do more damage—because they open the dialogue aimlessly.

Too often, you wait until you're talking to figure out what you want to say. You're good with takeoff—that is, initiating discussion—but you don't know how to land the plane. So you struggle and talk in circles until you finally discover what you want to say. You wait until the very end of a ten-minute monologue to deliver your "I say all of that to say . . ."

But by then it's often too late, and you lose the chance to connect.

The more topics, elements, or themes you pile onto a conversation, the more you weigh it down, and the less chance you have of it going anywhere. Without a clear frame or endpoint from the start, the conversation can quickly tire out the other person. The longer it takes to make your point, the more you waste the other person's diminishing attention. You'll lose them.

If you've ever heard someone respond with any of these questions, chances are you didn't put a frame around the conversation:

- "So, you don't want to go to the party?" (when you do)

- "What's your point?" (when you thought you already made it)

- "What are you wanting me to do?" (when you don't want them to do anything)

Often, these types of questions prompt you to yell out, "You're missing the point!" or "You're not listening to me!" But the questions to ask yourself are: Have I made my point easy to find? Have I put a frame around it to make it clear and concise? Or have I forced my listener to find a needle in a haystack?

Unclear parameters leave the other person playing the detective, and that can be a terribly frustrating experience. They're listening to you ramble and meander, all the while wondering where this is going. The other person may have no clue where the subject is coming from, what it's really about, or what you're ultimately asking of them. These unanswered questions pull one of the worst psychological triggers: fear of the unknown.

The fear of the unknown injects anxiety into conversations, particularly for people who are prone to immediately go to worst-case scenarios when conversations don't have defined space. Loss also becomes a trigger, as the other person fears they've done something wrong or that you want to exit the relationship.

These fears ramp up their ignition phase, causing overemotional reactions or launches into aggression, like shouting, "I don't know what you want!" Or it puts you in the position of asking them, "Why are you so upset? I'm just trying to talk to you!"

The problem lies in the undefined parameters. Without knowing why you're bringing it up, they're left twisting in the wind, wondering how it ends or if the hammer will drop. There's no understanding, no acknowledgment. And certainly no connection.

Now, keep in mind, you also need to know what a frame **isn't**. Adding a frame around a conversation doesn't mean:

- You get to dictate the conversation without room for their input or concern

- They're not allowed to disagree with you or defend themself
- Your frame is fair to them
- You can leave the frame when it suits you
- You're the only one who gets to speak your mind

Your frame for the conversation applies to you just as much as it does to the other person. It lets you, as well as the person across from you, know exactly what to expect, with clear purpose and little room for confusion. Another way to think of this is as mapping your conversation. If you want another person to travel with you from point A to point B, you need to tell them what your destination is, and you need to remove any anxiety they may have in getting there.

How to Frame a Conversation

As soon as you begin your next conversation, frame it first. Don't wait to try to set a frame just because they said something you don't like. That's not fair. Set the frame from the very start of the conversation. Here are each of the steps, followed by examples so you can hear exactly what framing a conversation sounds like.

1. Set a direction

Begin by telling the other person exactly what you want to speak about. Your words should be tailored to your conversational goal and values. For example:

- "I want to speak with you about your comments at yesterday's meeting."
- "I'd like to visit about salary expectations."
- "I need to discuss plans for Tuesday afternoon."
- "I'd like to talk with you about a subject personal to me."

2. Call your shot

Next, tell the other person how you want the conversation to end. You're projecting the intended result and setting the direction of the conversation. Detail exactly how you want to feel after the conversation is over. Be as specific as you can. To help, pretend you're finishing the phrase "And by the end of it":

- ". . . I want to walk away with us having a stronger working relationship."
- ". . . I want to leave with us knowing we still respect each other."
- ". . . I want to be heard without you feeling like you need to fix it."
- ". . . I want you to know that I still love you and want to be together."

3. Get their commitment

End the frame by securing their consent to the conversation. For example:

- "That sound good to you?"
- "Can we agree to that?"
- "Is that doable for you?"

Now let's see all three steps in action.

Imagine you're speaking to a colleague in a private area of the office coffee lounge. Using all three steps of framing, your first few sentences might sound like this:

"Thanks for meeting me. I'd like to talk briefly about what you said during this morning's session, and I want to walk away with us having a better understanding of what's important to each other and how we can improve. That okay with you?"

Here's another.

"I appreciate you taking the time. I'd like to talk about the expectations for this quarter, and I want to leave feeling comfortable that we're committed to the same priorities. Sound good?"

One more, this time in a relationship context.

"I'd like to talk to you about how I perceived your behavior last night, and I'm not saying anyone is right or wrong. I want to move forward knowing how to show up for each other better. Can we do that?"

With bright-line parameters like these, they'll rarely say no.

This structure takes advantage of the natural benefits of a frame by defining what's included and excluding what isn't. That is, the frame enhances what's inside the conversation and sets aside what's outside the conversation.

A frame also tells the other person that there will, in fact, be an end. Because the conversation now has a scope, the frame also enhances listening because the other person doesn't have to listen for anything else. Ultimately, frames strengthen the connection between sender and receiver.

One frame, one issue

"Okay, everyone, we have a lot to cover today," your boss begins.

Immediately, everyone in the meeting wants to groan or roll their eyes. Why? Because this opening sets the stage for a scattered, potentially overwhelming discussion in which focus is diluted across too many subjects. Just because there's an agenda doesn't mean it's an effective or an engaging one.

Ugh, you might think. **This could've been an email. This is a waste of time.** Deep down, you know that most of the issues won't get covered (or covered well). You also know that the meeting will likely result in another meeting. You don't feel confident that there will be outcomes, action steps, or takeaways—only people meeting to say they met and talking to say they talked. It's hard to create a strong connection when the signal is spread so thin.

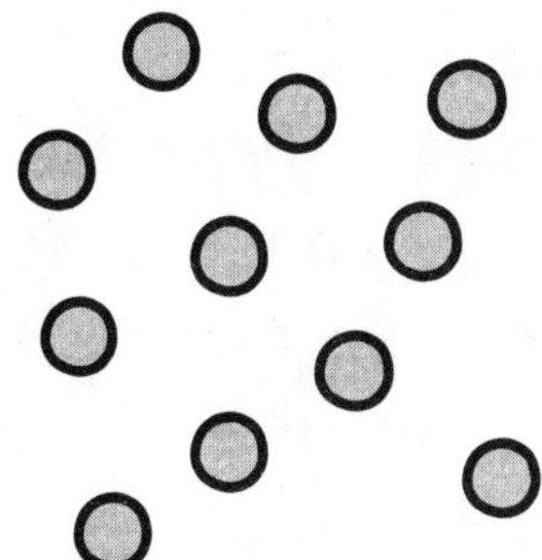

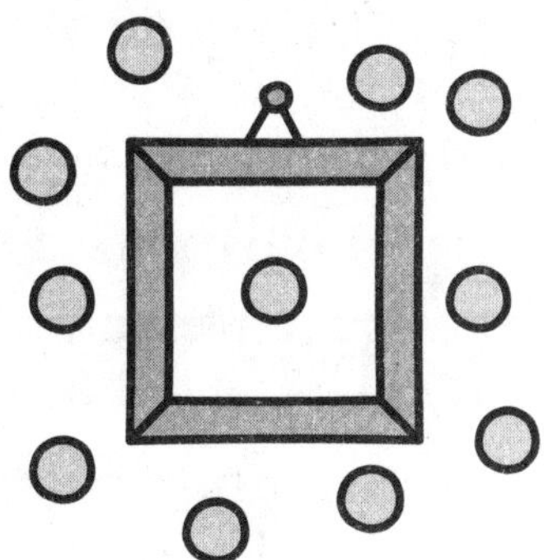

ISSUE

That's why you need a framework of one frame, one issue.

Imagine if your manager were to start with this: "Today, we're focusing on improving our client feedback process." You'd likely feel more engaged and clearer about the meeting's purpose. This specificity narrows everyone's focus. When the meeting ends and the topic has been covered, everyone leaves happier because the conversation felt more productive and meaningful and worth their time.

"One frame, one issue" is important for keeping discussions concise and on track. When a conversation has just one frame, two benefits occur:

1. You're forced to eliminate the fluff by synthesizing and placing intentional effort into precisely what you need to say.

2. You create deeper space for more thoughtful discussion on the topic at hand.

When you're not bouncing from one issue to another, there's a chance to go beneath the surface. There's more room to explore nuances, consider various perspectives, and collaborate on solutions. "One frame, one issue" encourages everyone involved to be present and engaged rather than mentally preparing for the next topic on a lengthy agenda.

In practice, applying this ratio might mean breaking down a meeting with a broad scope into several smaller, punchier micro sessions. Or when texting or emailing, it could mean addressing a single concern per message to the right decision-makers rather than lumping multiple threads or topics into one reply-all communication.

Remember, clarity is kind. This method respects everyone's time and cognitive resources and leads to tighter connections.

How to Nudge a Conversation Back into View

It happens. It's nobody's fault, but somehow the conversation bled out of the original frame you set. Maybe you simply got off topic or went down a rabbit hole. It's innocent. Understand that it's also totally okay to let conversations explore themselves naturally. If it gets to be a problem, the easy trick to get back on track is to use the keyword of your goal.

For example, maybe you both got sidetracked discussing your mutual disdain for Gary in accounting when you were supposed to be talking about the marketing budget. A quick use of the word **marketing** can bring you back to center. Or you can state the obvious with "We're getting off track." No harm done.

But sometimes it's not that innocent. Sensitive conversations can quickly fall into personal attacks or bring up past grievances that are a deterrent to the current goal. This tactic is often used, intentionally or unintentionally, to deflect from the issue or to gain an upper hand in an incoming argument. When this happens, it's critical to recognize the shift away from productive dialogue and to steer the conversation back into frame.

Let's look at two different scenarios to illustrate. In scenario one, you're the person who took the conversation to a bad place. You said something you shouldn't have said and now things are looking worse. For that, you need to make three moves quickly:

1. Apologize for what you said that derailed the conversation.
   a. "I'm sorry. I shouldn't have said that."
   b. "I'm sorry I raised my voice."

2. Follow it up with words that convey distance from the goal.
    a. "That was unhelpful."
    b. "That wasn't fair."
    c. "That's not what you agreed to."

3. Immediately pick up where you left off before things went south.

Here's what that can look like all together: "Hey, I'm sorry. I shouldn't have raised my voice. That wasn't helpful, and it's not what you agreed to. I'm wanting to understand how we can prevent what happened yesterday from happening again."

In scenario two, the other person derails the conversation. It's a common defensive tactic that, when left unchecked, will rapidly turn a conversation into an argument. Let's assume you want to discuss an off moment that happened at a friend's house. You've set your frame, and your friend has agreed. But fifteen minutes in, your friend pops off with a tangent: "Oh really? **Really?** That's what you're going with? What about when you did the same thing three weeks ago?"

Comments like this are a product of the other person's ignition phase: they want the spotlight to move off them. They'll typically try to do one of two things:

1. Put the attention on you and divert it away from them

2. Level the playing field by bringing something up (usually the past) that attempts to equate their behavior with yours, in a sort of "you too" comeback

When your next conversation falls out of frame in this way, it's crucial that you engage control of your body to minimize your ignition phase. To keep the discussion from spiraling, and with calm, controlled words and a conversational breath, try these phrases:

1. "I hear your point. I need to finish the conversation we started. And if needed, I'm willing to come back and address that comment."

2. "Stay with me. Hear me out, and if we need to come back to that we can."

3. "I agree that's worth talking about too. Let's focus on one issue at a time."

The key to these approaches is first acknowledging what they said, then controlling your response in a way that refocuses you on the topic. What you cannot do is dismiss their comments with something like "That's beside the point!" or "You're just deflecting." Dismissive words like these will only ensure that you're introducing another layer to the conflict, whether the comment was beside the point or whether they're trying to deflect. That leads nowhere good. So remember. Acknowledge, then hold.

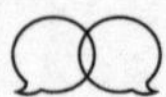

Frames are powerful tools for connecting in conversations both big and small. The next time you're in a meeting or discussion and you feel like you're talking in circles or getting nowhere, try using a frame. Choose one issue. Set a direction. Call your shot. And get their commitment. You'll decrease distractions and minimize misunderstanding. You'll increase attention and connection. You'll accomplish more in less time. And the other person will see you as someone who respects both their time and insight.

CHAPTER SUMMARY

- The more issues you raise in a conversation, the less likely you'll feel that the conversation was productive or that anything was accomplished.
- To connect to the other person, you need to ensure that you're always speaking toward one purpose and direction.
- To prevent unhelpful tangents or misinterpretations, place a frame around the

conversation before it starts. That means if you want to take someone from A to B, you first need to tell them and remove the anxiety of what B looks like.

- Frame your conversation by first telling them what you want to talk about; then tell them what you want to feel after you talk about it; last, get their commitment to go in that direction together.

- When you apply a frame to the conversation, you reduce the chances of misunderstanding and improve the likelihood of reaching your connection goals.

CHAPTER 11

Defensiveness

"It's a matter of vector forces, frankly, the influence of which is mostly all but unseen to the untrained eye," said the opposing party's biomechanical engineer on the witness stand.

His job was to testify that the vehicle that hit my client at fifty-six miles per hour couldn't have caused a bodily injury—or at the most, a very minor one.

My job on cross-examination was to disprove that opinion.

He didn't like my question. And I didn't care for his answer.

Expert witnesses in a trial can make or break a case. You need them because there are certain things that can be said only by people who have legally sufficient knowledge about a subject, like accident reconstruction or forensic analysis, to give an opinion. The easy part is getting an expert to talk. The harder part is getting them to stop. Experts tend to speak in a way that highlights their intelligence. Good experts allow everyone in the courtroom to understand their testimony, making it relevant and accessible. Bad experts use technical jargon to make others feel small. The expert I had on cross-examination was of the latter type.

"Yessir, I understand what you're saying," I replied. "I'm going to ask it differently."

After a pause, I continued. "You're testifying on behalf of the defendant, the person who hit my client?"

"The person whose vehicle made contact with the subject vehicle, yessir," he responded.

See what I mean?

"The person who hit my client had to be taken away by ambulance?" I said.

"Uh, I believe so, I'm not certain," he said hesitantly.

"For a broken collarbone?" I pressed.

Clearing his throat, he replied, "Again, that—that may be true."

I pressed more. "And you're telling this jury that this accident couldn't have caused disc herniations to my client's back?"

It was a question meant to put him on the spot. The kind of question that makes a juror look up from their notepad to pay close attention to what will come next. Now, what this expert could've said was something like "No, not exactly. My opinion is more nuanced than that." Or even better,

"That does sound contradictory, I agree. But it's not as simple as that." A response like that would've sounded reasonable. In fact, it would've made him look more credible by acknowledging the distinction I was making and using it to support his point. Instead, this is what the jury heard:

"Well, sir," he said, adjusting his glasses and sitting up straight to sharpen his tone, "that requires a more thorough discussion of physics and human biology, if you can grasp it."

The energy in the air changed immediately as the jury rustled in their chairs. One female juror, an older lady, shook her head in disapproval and whispered, "Mm-mm. My lawd."

The expert did the one thing you never want to do in front of a jury. He took my question as a challenge to his expertise, and he got defensive. His defensiveness, in turn, made his opinion look less believable. It was a crucial moment when, instead of bridging the gap and connecting his opinion and the jury's understanding, he widened it with his own ego.

And while this single moment certainly didn't dismantle his whole testimony, it eroded the trust the defense needed the jury to have in him. In a trial, where every word of testimony on the record matters, the ability to communicate the evidence is just as significant as the evidence itself—for good or for bad. Here, everyone in the courtroom saw it: the expert's defensiveness not only undermined his own argument but also highlighted a major weakness in the defense's entire case.

Defensive behavior isn't unique to expert witnesses. It applies to everyone. You. Me. From the courtroom to the living room. Defensiveness can show up at any time. Recognizing when you're being defensive, knowing why it's happening—and arming yourself with the tools to manage it—can transform the trust others place in you.

Why Defensiveness Breaks Connection

There is little that's more costly to your next conversation than the price of defensiveness.

Someone getting defensive is the most telltale sign of a spark of the ignition phase. Everything shuts down. Shields go up. Spikes come out. Backs turn and earmuffs go on. Defensiveness is the suit of armor you put on when you feel triggered. It's a stress response that takes many forms. Maybe it's the feeling of a knot in your stomach or a tenseness behind your ears. Maybe it manifests as sarcasm, silent treatment, or even laughing off serious topics. But day-to-day, when you get defensive, here's what you'll often do:

- Interrupt: "Yeah, but you didn't even . . ."
- Raise your voice: "You can't actually be serious!"

- Resort to a personal attack: "You're such an idiot."

- Dismiss their view without hearing them out: "Pfft. You don't even care."

- Deflect with past grievances: "Well, what about the time that you . . ."

- Generalize: "You never listen to me!" or "You always do this!"

Sound familiar? I'm betting so.

Now read them again. What do they all have in common?

You.

It's the first word that wants to come out of your mouth when the shields go up. It's the first person in the crosshairs of your pointed index finger when you're giving a piece of your mind. So what if I said that? So what if I did something wrong? "Oh, **me**? What about you?"

This reflex of pointing outward instead of inward highlights a fundamental feature of human communication: the deep-seated aversion to being wrong or perceived as flawed. Being thought of as wrong hits every psychological trigger:

- Social evaluation: If I'm wrong, will I be humiliated? Will they reject me?

- Personal identity: If I'm wrong, do I still matter? Am I defective?
- Loss: If I'm wrong, will they walk away? Will I lose my reputation?

Defensiveness Builds a Wall

The perception of threat raises your guard. The emotional overtakes the analytical as everything inside you wants to fight against or run from the threat posed by the other person. It's enough to make you want to put them on mute, with fingers in your ears, taunting "la la la." You don't want to listen. You don't want to learn. You don't want to reason.

When you're on the other end of defensive behavior, it can be maddening. No matter what you say or how you try to say it, they just won't listen. Try changing their mind as much as you'd like. It won't work, because the harder you try to prove them wrong, the more convinced they are that they're right.

The number one reason that people (myself included) refuse to listen is because they're uncomfortable. What I've said conflicts with what you believe, and that creates discomfort. That discomfort is called cognitive dissonance—that unpleasant feeling you get when new information clashes with your existing beliefs. The feeling can come from any source: engaging in heated debate, reading an article on the internet, or even hearing the lyrics to a song. Often, it stems from big societal or political questions, the type that candidates will make their campaigns about. It's why people tend to religiously stick to a single news source and dismiss views from any other channels. But it can occur with the little things too, like having to order something else on the menu when the restaurant is out of your usual, or hearing that a new brand of coffee is better than the one you've been drinking for years. Things that are different can feel threatening and ignite psychological triggers.

See, what you and I believe is rarely our own but is tied to or passed on by people we love, or memories we cherish that have created our identity. That means if I were to tell you that you're wrong about a given belief, like political ideology, I'd most likely not just be saying that you're wrong. I could be saying your grandmother is wrong, your best friend is wrong, or that memory you've had since you were ten is wrong.

And you'd do anything—even to the point of refusing to listen—to avoid that discomfort. That's why logic doesn't work. More proof doesn't automatically lead to more acceptance. Instead, it can lead to digging your heels in deeper, not only defending your own stance but also protecting your relationships and the narratives that shape who you are. You become defensive to "take up" for the entity you've made a part of you—the trigger of identity by association you learned about in chapter four. And the harder I work against you, to push my point in your face, the more hardened you'll become.

Your defensiveness, while a natural mechanism designed to protect you, often does more harm than good. By putting up walls, two things happen:

1. You prevent others from understanding you.
2. You shut yourself off from understanding them.

And here's the problem. You accept the consequences of number two, but dismiss the consequences of number one. Meaning you drop all expectations of yourself, and at the same time maintain all the expectations of the other person. You still expect them to understand you. You still expect them to cater to your feelings. It's like locking your door and then getting upset that the other person hasn't come inside yet. I'm sure you've heard yourself or someone say, "They should know." They should know I'm upset. They should know how that would affect me. These are the same people who, when the shoe is on the other foot, shout, "I can't read your mind!"

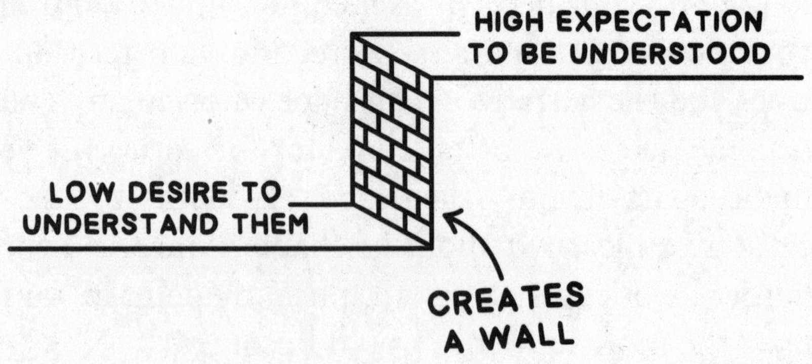

Don't convince yourself that this cycle is a symptom of one person. Everyone does it. When you're a pedestrian crossing the street, you think, "These cars can wait on me. I'm the pedestrian. Can't they see that I'm walking?" But when you're a driver stopped at an intersection, you think, "Look at all these pedestrians . . . just walking around like they own the place. I think this guy is walking slower on purpose. Can't they see that I'm driving?" This shift in perspective illustrates how quickly you allow your sympathies to adjust, yet you expect the sympathies of those around you to remain fixed.

From a technical view, what you're feeling is what psychologists call fundamental attribution error, which influences your understanding or judgment of others. Fundamental attribution error describes the concept that you tend to overemphasize personality-based explanations and underemphasize external situational factors. For example, if you see someone walking into the office late, you might paint them as a lazy, uncaring, or unmotivated person (personality-based explanation) and minimize factors like heavy traffic, bad weather, or a personal matter (situational explanation). And if that person were to walk by you without saying hi, you may think they did it on purpose.

That's another major problem with using "you." It leads you to take things personally, so you interpret others' words or actions as a direct attack on you even when they may not be. Consider this example. You and your spouse are in the kitchen.

YOU: "What's up with you? You seem out of it."

SPOUSE: "I'm overwhelmed. It's been a long day, the house is a mess, and the last thing I want to do is clean these dishes."

YOU: "You're saying that I don't help out around here? I did the dishes yesterday."

SPOUSE: "That's not what I'm saying."

YOU: "That's absolutely what you're saying. You think that I don't do enough around here. When it's me who makes sure the house is picked up. It's me that makes sure schedules run on time."

Oof. See what I mean? There's no chance for connection.

When the walls go up, you care less about trying to understand the other person yet expect them to care more about trying to understand you. Your spouse was trying to open up about their day. Instead of using that opportunity to connect, you unilaterally chose to turn it into an indictment of your character.

Here's another one that often draws out the spikes.

Someone responds to your four-sentence text with "Ok," or worse, "K."

The first thought you have is, "What do you mean, 'Ok'? What kind of 'Ok' is that?"

You may get in your head about it. **"Ok"? Just "Ok"? That's all the effort he cared to put into that text? That's so rude**, you think to yourself. You may be tempted to show the text to another person to get assurance—"Isn't that just so rude?" You decide to send a reply.

"You know what, just forget it. I don't need this right now."

Miscommunication escalates into an argument, and for the rest of the evening, your time is railroaded by an argument that never had to happen. Turns out, the "Ok" was the result of a rushed response while they were at the checkout counter but still wanted to show that they acknowledged your text.

When you take things personally, you create a self-fulfilling prophecy. Let's use the text scenario to illustrate:

- You perceive the text as rude, receiving it as a personal attack on you.

- That perception triggers the emotional reactions of your ignition phase.

- Now driven by your emotions, you respond defensively.

- Your response causes the other person to respond defensively.
- The cycle now reinforces and fulfills your belief that you are, in fact, under attack.

This cycle frequently happens with written communication via text, email, or instant messaging, in which vocal nuance is lost. It's part of confirmation bias, in which you tend to seek out information that confirms or reinforces your existing belief while rejecting information that doesn't. That means once you allow your trigger to control you, you begin to selectively look for information that feeds that trigger and dismiss the information that deprives it. For instance, if you're complaining to someone that they forgot to do something, you might focus on the times when they didn't do it and dismiss all the times that they did. You look for the negative and reject the positive because it reinforces your defensive behavior.

How to Stop Defensiveness

But there's a cure.

It begins with understanding that how often you take things personally is a direct reflection of how much grace you give other people. How freely you give the benefit of the doubt.

The more open you are to the idea that someone's actions or words might not be intended as a personal slight, the less likely you are to feel offended by them. This grace—this willingness to see beyond yourself—can transform how you interact with the world. When you hold back on giving the benefit of the doubt, you also hold back on giving ease to your own peace of mind.

When you offer grace, on the other hand, you allow for the possibility that the waitress's curt response was the result of frustration because she was supposed to get off by six p.m. and her mother is watching her kids; the car in front of you is going slow (i.e., going the speed limit) because the driver just lost his wife of fifty-three-years last week; your manager sent a short email because she's juggling not only her life but also the life of her older brother who just got out of rehab—and not because she meant anything at all toward you. Remember, the person you see is not the person you're talking to.

When you take things personally, you're picking up what no one has asked you to carry. Put it down and assume positive intent until proven otherwise.

The intentional practice of empathy and kindness will fundamentally alter how you treat yourself. You'll become more forgiving and less critical of your own mistakes, and ultimately a happier person to be around.

Whereas taking things personally results in self-fulfilling negativity, giving grace results in self-fulfilling **positivity**.

This is your wake-up call. It's time you take

ownership of your words and realize that not everything that is said requires a response from you. Maybe you forgot, but you get to decide if what somebody says means anything to you. You get to decide whether you take what they did personally. You get to decide the weight or value that you put on their words. And too often what somebody says isn't worth the paper if you wrote it down, yet you hold it and collect it. And before you know it, you're carrying a bag of books.

Stop carrying the weight of other people's words.

Stop attending every argument you're invited to.

If sports are your jam, just because they throw a pitch doesn't mean you have to swing. Let it go by. Just because they hit it to your side of the court doesn't mean you have to send it back over the net. Let it fall to the ground. There is no requirement, no compulsion, that just because they said something, you are obligated to say anything at all.

"I just have to say . . ." No, you don't.

There's nothing you have to say. There are only things you want to say. But who are you saying it for? Are you saying it to make a point? Or are you just saying it to be heard?

Accountability of defensiveness means recognizing your impulse to point outward and choosing instead to point inward. I use the word **choose** because that's what it is. It's a choice. And that choice is yours.

Here's how to stop yourself from getting defensive.

1. Catch yourself

Prevent the knee-jerk reaction of having something to say with a conversational breath (a nine-second pause). Slow breathing tells your body that what someone said or did isn't a threat.

2. Let their words fall

In the silence of the pause, imagine that their words don't reach you but fall to the ground. Resist the urge to "catch" them and throw them back. Imagining the words falling to the ground gives you the chance to consider whether it's worth your time to pick them up or leave them alone. If you feel the pull to get defensive, remind yourself with the phrase "Put it down, [your name]."

3. Get curious

Turn your mind from outward to inward and keep your analytical side engaged. Ask yourself questions like: Where is this coming from? What is driving them to say this? What information am I missing? Get in the habit of becoming curious about the source of the request or statement.

Once you have better control of yourself, there are three strategies you can use to help prevent the other person from getting defensive. While these techniques aren't foolproof, they will help you break down walls.

Here's how to prevent the other person from getting defensive.

1. Begin your sentence with "I," not "You"

As soon as you start your sentence with **you**, it automatically puts the other person in a defensive stance. When you start your sentence with **I**, you prevent their trigger because it focuses on your feelings and perspective, not on notions that you're accusing or blaming them. It's also a more assertive approach.

For example:

- Instead of "You're always looking at your phone."
  - Try "I enjoy sharing time together without our screens."

- Rather than "You don't appreciate me."
  - Try "I felt unappreciated when you didn't respond."

- Instead of "You can't speak to me that way!"
  - Try "I don't respond to that."

2. Don't begin your question with "Why?"

In most scenarios in which you're questioning someone, **why** comes across as accusatory. It often implies wrongdoing, blame, or judgment. It hits their autonomy trigger. Imagine driving your car with a friend in the passenger seat. As you take a different route on the way to their house, your friend scowls and asks, "Why'd you go this way?" Your gut instinct is to push back. "Why? Because I wanted to, that's why," you want to say. Or to your toddler who repeats "Why?" over and over again, making you want to yell, "Because I said so!"

It's not that they're asking you a question that upsets you. It's that "why" feels like they're questioning **you**. To fix it, replace the "why" with "what," "when," or "how."

- Instead of "Why didn't you take the trash out?"
  - Try "When are you planning on taking out the trash?"

- Rather than "Why'd you do it like that?"
  - Try "How did you decide on this?"

- Instead of "Why can't you just relax?"
  - Try "What's preventing you from relaxing?"

3. Acknowledge first

People have a deep desire to feel heard. When you respond to their point with "Yeah but," it only makes matters worse because it sends the message that you're not acknowledging them. And if you don't acknowledge them, believe me, they'll return the favor. Their door will be shut with the curtains drawn. Instead, simply try validating their feelings or perspective before presenting your own. This approach keeps their door open for dialogue.

For example:

- **Tell them what you agree with.** Now, this doesn't mean that you have to agree with anything that they said. Instead of thinking micro, think macro. You can agree that the discussion should be had, that the topic is worth talking about, or that the decision needs to be made.
    - For example: "I agree this topic is worth discussing."

- **Tell them what you've learned.** When you state that you've learned something, the other person will feel like they've taught something. Telling them what you've learned makes them feel like they contributed to the discussion and that you're acknowledging their insight.
    - For example: "I've learned that this subject is very important to you."

- **Tell them that they're helpful.** People like to feel helpful, especially if they can help themselves. When you acknowledge that they've helped you, they're more likely to remain more open and

forthcoming. You free their defensiveness with acknowledgment.
- For example: "That's helpful to know."

Connecting to the other person means you have to be aware of the walls all around you, both the ones you build and the ones built against you. When you feel yourself getting defensive, get quiet, then get curious. When you feel someone else getting defensive, change your words from those that put up walls to those that break them down. It's a shift toward a connection mindset that opens up to more understanding and acknowledgment, rather than confrontation and the urge to win.

CHAPTER SUMMARY

- Becoming defensive is the quickest way to break connection between you and the other person, a bright-line indicator that you're entering your ignition phase.

- Defensive behavior, from either of you, puts up a wall. It stops the other person from understanding you, and it closes you off from understanding the other person.

- Prevent yourself from getting defensive by using a long pause, five to ten seconds, to maintain your cooling phase. Imagine their words falling to the ground before they reach you and resist the urge to pick them up.

- Defuse the defensiveness of others by beginning your response with "I" and not "you." Use phrases that first acknowledge what they said, instead of immediately responding with your own position.

- When you learn not to attend every argument you're invited to, you can prevent the wall from coming between you and the other person and preserve connection.

CHAPTER 12

Difficult Conversations

Conversations about the hard stuff aren't easy. That's why I saved this chapter for last.

Chances are you're reading this book because your next conversation may be a difficult one. And if that's the case, I'm grateful you're here and that you've made it this far.

It tells me that you've accepted the challenge to break the cycle. You've chosen to stop seeing arguments as something to win and instead see them as an opportunity to understand the person behind the words. You're building the discipline to connect to the person in front of you.

By now you know that it all starts with what you say next.

How you handle a difficult conversation says more about your character than the content of the conversation itself. Whether it's breaking up with a significant other, firing an employee, talking about finances, or addressing the elephant in the room, how you enter the conversation is the most important part. Like the calm before the storm, remember?

If you come in too hot and heavy-handed, the other person will withdraw and get defensive ("Me? What about you?!"). If you come in too soft and unassuming, they'll become suspicious of your motives ("What are you trying to say?"). And if you're too passive and shy, they might just run right over you ("I'm not listening to this.").

A difficult conversation becomes more difficult for one of two reasons:

1. You don't know where you're going.
2. You don't know how to get there.

What if I told you that I once hopped on a plane but didn't know where it was going to land? Or that I started driving but had no clue when I was going to stop? You'd think I was nuts. But it happens all the time in our conversations. When you just expect the conversation to go how you played it out in your mind—without any idea of where you're going and how you'll get there—you're setting yourself up for disappointment, as discussed in chapter two.

The best time to remove the difficult from a difficult conversation is before it even starts. Approach is everything.

Your approach to a difficult conversation makes the difference between creating connection or losing it forever. What follows is a blueprint for building connection when the going gets tough. Side note: this chapter assumes that you've already done the work from previous chapters to gain control of your emotions and hone your assertive voice. Once you're prepared to say it with control and say it with confidence, then and only then will you be ready to say it to connect.

Here are three rules to ensure that your approach lands smoothly every time.

1. Set aside real, undistracted time

I learned this rule the hard way.

I was clerking (law-speak for "interning") under a partner at a firm while still in law school. I had a question about part of an assignment I was struggling with, and I was embarrassed to ask him. I stewed and struggled all morning before mustering up the courage to go and speak with him. I got up from my desk, walked down the hall, and headed straight into the partner's office. Without thinking, I knocked twice on his open door and started speaking right as I walked through his doorway.

"Hey, I have a question about the motion for—" I began, walking into the center of the room.

"Nope! Out!" he shouted, his left hand lifted in a talk-to-the-hand position.

I turned on a swivel and walked straight out with the same speed I'd walked in with. Before I left, I caught a glimpse of him typing intently on his computer. Embarrassed, I sat back down at my desk with ears red and burning. I knew better. About fifteen minutes later, I heard a knock. The partner was standing in the doorway.

"May I come in?" he asked.

"Of course," I said, my ears finally returning to a normal color.

"Sorry about that. My mind was right in the middle of something. If I didn't finish it then, I was going to forget my thought. Whatcha got?" he asked.

I took a big gulp and told him about my confusion.

"Ah," he said, smiling. "Yeah, I know why you were confused. I made a typo. I'll fix that. And next time, just shoot me an email suggesting a time to visit. That way I can help when I'm at a stopping place."

The problem wasn't the topic. The problem was my timing.

If you're going to have a difficult conversation, remove the external factors that make it more difficult: find a private and comfortable setting, choose a time when neither of you is rushed or stressed, and eliminate any potential interruptions.

When you force conversations to happen within your time frame, the other person often goes into it unwillingly from the outset. It's like driving at seventy miles per hour on a highway only to have a slower car merge right in front of you, forcing you to put on your brakes. It ruins your momentum and your focus.

Now swap roles. There are few things more frustrating than when someone tries to force you into a conversation you're not ready for. Sometimes, the fact that you're not ready to have the conversation is what makes it difficult. You'll feel pressured and more prone to stress responses. It's a product of your autonomy trigger. They're pushing a conversation on you when it's not a good time. As a result, you'll have a harder time grasping clearer thoughts because your emotions are telling you that you don't feel comfortable. You may find yourself asking them to repeat what they said or go over it again. Your mind doesn't have a clean space on its desk to work from.

Instead, set an assigned time in the future to have the discussion.

The next time you need to schedule a talk, try this:

- "When would be a good time Friday morning to go over . . . ?"

- "Do you have a window around one forty-five on Tuesday to discuss . . . ?"

- "Are you available Thursday night to talk about . . . ?"

I like to use the words **capacity** and **bandwidth**.

- "Do you have capacity to talk about Monday's meeting agenda this afternoon?"

- "Do you have the bandwidth to talk about the kids' schedule for tomorrow once they go down for bed?"

It speaks not only to their capacity of time but also to their capacity of mind. Sure, they may have the time, but they may not have the emotional or mental bandwidth to take it on at that time. There are lots of different ways to ask, so find one that feels most comfortable to you.

The key is to suggest a narrow time frame or a particular time of the day. Even if you're free to talk and they're free to talk at that very moment, it's almost always better to set the meeting in the future. You need time to sift through your thoughts. More so, you want to give the other person time to prepare themselves. Have you ever had someone pop by your office and say, "Hey, you got a second? I mean not right now but later. Just need to visit about a thought." Whew. It's almost a relief. Later is good. Just half an hour can do wonders for ensuring that you have ample time to ready yourself to say what you need to say with control. So set the discussion for the future, and preferably with a narrow time frame.

Remember, the fewer choices you give, the easier it becomes for people to decide. If you just say, "So, when is a good time next week?" you'll likely hear back, "I'm not sure. I'll get back to you." Next thing you know, three weeks have gone by. But if you narrow the scope, you're more likely to get an answer and work toward a mutual time frame. It's not a hard-and-fast rule, but it does help.

By the way, here's how you don't want to set aside time:

- "I need to talk to you."
- "Got a second?"
- "When are you free later?"

Again, consider how you feel when someone approaches you like that.

Additionally, none of these examples provides any reference to meaningful time. While you may like that they suggest a lack of urgency, the more harmful effect is uncertainty. **Do you have a second to talk?** It depends. Is the topic positive or negative, personal or professional, serious or trivial? Each of these factors affects your response. You might have a few seconds for the other person to tell you about a funny thing that happened last night—if that story actually lasts a few seconds. That's a big if. Typically, the "Got a second?" line should more aptly be worded, "Got two hours?" Set clear expectations to ensure that the time you requested for conversation respects the topic it will hold. Serious topics need more time. Sensitive topics need more time. Negative topics need more time. It helps to tell someone if you need thirty minutes, or an hour, or four hours.

By improving your ability to forecast how much you need of someone's time and to set that intentional time aside, you're positioning yourself for better connection. How? Because you're building in time for intentional pauses, as well as for stretches of silence for thinking and keeping the conversation within your frame. It offers you time for slow breathing and slower words to keep you controlled and clearheaded.

Conversely, if you don't forecast the time requirements and rush into the conversation, you might find yourself talking to someone who's more concerned about when they're getting out of the conversation than the substance of the conversation.

Make sure the time you've set aside is undistracted. Don't have your phone on your desk (it doesn't count if it's face down). Don't hold your phone in your hand (it doesn't count if you're not looking at it). Send the message that what you have to discuss is your singular focus.

2. Drop the pleasantries

Imagine that you need to let go of a member of your team. You've tried for weeks to give this person a chance, but it's time for the two of you to part ways. You send this email: "Please come see me in my office when you have a second."

In your mind, you're thinking that you'll have the discussion in a few hours or so. But nope. The employee walks into your office barely two minutes after you hit send. She looks nervous. She knows her work hasn't been great despite her attempts to improve.

"Oh, hello!" you say cheerfully, letting out a nervous cough. "Take a seat."

A few seconds go by as you begin slightly touching things around your desk and resort to fidgeting with a lone paper clip.

"How are you?" you ask. "How are you liking it here?"

"I love it." She forces a smile. "I feel totally supported and just really like my job. It's taken much longer than I'd hoped, but I feel like I'm about to hit my stride."

Ugh. You weren't prepared for that. You twist awkwardly and readjust yourself in your seat. In the quiet, her smile starts to fade as she's searching for her next words.

You manage to press on. "Hey, uh, listen." The air drops from the room. "So I've been doing a lot of thinking, and it's been a very hard decision for me. Because I like you, and I think you're a great person. And I know you try hard. I hate to tell you this. But I, uh, I think it's, uh, time to let you go."

Instantly, her tears well up. You turn your eyes downward.

She pleads, "But why? I like it here and . . ."

And what you originally planned to be a five-minute conversation turns into an hour-and-a-half discussion that ends with you giving her two more weeks on the team—a move you're sure you'll regret.

When the topic of conversation is truly a touchy subject or will be received as bad news, we're tempted to create a soft atmosphere. To soften the blow. To let them down easy. This typically starts by asking about the other person's day, or their family, or by drumming up some random topic you've never taken any interest in before ("Do you garden?" Womp). You think you're making things better. That you're being kind or tactful.

But people are smarter than that.

Despite your incredible acting skills, people have an innate ability to sense a threat. Something feels . . . off. People are really good at reading nonverbal cues. You can sense when someone is watching you. You know when someone has entered a room even if your eyes are shut. And you can feel the tension before an argument, as discussed in chapter five. A moment of insincerity from you and the other person will immediately put up their guard. Their ignition phase puts them on alert. At any moment, they're ready and expecting the hammer to drop.

Your team member felt it. Not only did you not set aside time for the discussion, you also led with pleasantries. She already knew that her work performance had been struggling. She knew full well what you wanted to speak to her about. She knew why she was there. She could sense by your fidgeting and readjusting in your seat that you were uncomfortable. As innocent as your "How are you?" was meant to be, it became disingenuous. You didn't really care how she was or how she liked it here. You were planning on firing her.

While harmless on the surface, opening with pleasantries feigns concern. It will create the opposite effect you want: instead of treating them with kindness, you are treating them with disguised indifference. Firing an employee, addressing a tough issue in a relationship, or sharing your feelings that you've kept locked up for weeks—it doesn't matter. People want honesty. Direct, true honesty. And the further you keep that from them, the more pretense they'll hear and the weaker your connection will be.

As best you can, drop these types of questions from your approach to difficult conversations:

- "So, how are you?"
- "What have you been up to lately?"
- "This weather needs to make up its mind, right?"

Instead, be direct and transparent from the outset. Begin the conversation by telling them what kind of conversation they're about to have. For bad news, try this:

- "This is going to be hard to hear."
- "I've got bad news."
- "You're not going to like what I have to say."
- "This might come as a shock to you."

Or, for tough or sensitive topics, try this:

- "This isn't going to be fun for either of us."
- "I have something uncomfortable to share."
- "This isn't going to be easy to talk about."

A simple "This is going to be a difficult conversation" works well too.

These types of statements should be the very first thing out of your mouth. Or, at a minimum, they should follow you saying, "Thank you for making time to talk with me." This type of approach is more open and honest. And yes, even though it feels more uncomfortable or distressing, it's kinder. Their system doesn't have to guess and wrestle with the unknown.

Let's look at what a more direct conversation could have looked like with your team member.

"Thanks for coming in," you begin.

She sits down.

You look at her and calmly say, "This is going to be difficult to hear."

After giving her a one-second pause to ready herself for your next words, you continue, "I need to let you go."

She nods in acknowledgment.

"We've enjoyed your time with us, and I'm excited to see where your career takes you." You finish with a warm grin.

"I understand," she responds, visibly disappointed. "Thank you for the opportunity."

Again, clarity is kind. It removes the ambiguity and anxiety that can cloud difficult conversations, allowing both of you to connect to the reality of the situation. When you allow the other person to receive difficult news with dignity, it reinforces their ability to handle the truth and empowers them with a more mature response.

3. Begin with your end

When you're having difficult conversations, lead with your takeaway. In other words, imagine that you're giving a presentation and you get to the end, the part where you say, "In **conclusion**." Move everything after that to the **front** of your conversation.

Let's assume you're in a meeting and giving out this idea: "Okay, so you know how we all want customers to feel comfortable once they get to the front desk? So I was thinking, and tell me if I'm wrong here, but too often we get into the whole concept of overcomplicating the customer experience, which is essentially just the idea that people don't know what they want, right? Okay, wait. I had this thought while I was driving and it hit me so randomly, I don't know why, but anyway. I say all that to say, we should totally simplify our approach and focus on creating a more welcoming environment in the lobby from the moment they enter."

Oof.

Can you see how you don't really know where it's going or what the ultimate ask will be until you're at the end?

Listeners get lost. They'll hook onto a word like **driving** and go into a mental rabbit hole remembering what they were thinking about while driving into work. **I passed that new Italian restaurant driving to work this morning. I've been wanting to try it. And speaking of food, how much longer until lunch? What should I eat? I ate lasagna yesterday. . . .**

And just like that, they're no longer in the room with you. They're thinking about their past, living in their future, and in no way concerned about their present.

Let's see what it looks like when you move the end to the beginning.

Sitting around the meeting table, you share your idea. "We should create a more welcoming environment for the lobby. If we make the entrance an inviting space, customers will be more likely to be comfortable by the time they get to the front desk."

That's it.

Now there's no chance the listener has gotten lost. No one is dreaming about pasta. You've immediately made your point and you've given your reasoning.

This technique works with written communication and text messages too. Combined with removing pleasantries and justifications, this puts you in a much better position. Imagine you have to turn down an invitation to a party. Which rejection sounds better?

- Text 1: Hey! Ok so I'm so sorry but I've just had sooo much to do today and I've been so stressed. I haven't even eaten yet lol. Turns out my dog had an allergic reaction to something and he's acting strange. I'm worried about him. I feel so so terrible but I may not be able to make it tonight. Thank you so much for thinking of me and if things change I'll definitely let you know!

- Text 2: I got bad news, I can't go tonight. Thank you for the invite. Hope it's a great time!

Text 1 sounds disingenuous. Despite your different attempts at not wanting to hurt their feelings, you've written so much that you leave the actual truth of what you mean up to their own making.

The more words you have to use, the more you sound like you're lying. You'd likely get a snarky text back of "Just tell me you don't want to come."

Text 2 gets straight to the point, making it sound more honest. It's a response that respects both you and the other person.

These strategies can help you start difficult conversations with other people. How can you be more open when it's someone else's turn to have a difficult conversation with you?

What It Means to Be a Safe Space

A few months ago, my six-year-old son walked into the living room toward me, head hanging down, his hands on top of his stomach.

"Daddy?" he said.

"What's up, buddy?" I asked.

"I did something bad," he replied as he moved his hands to show a two-inch hole in his new shirt.

"What happened?" I asked.

He looked down again. "I just wanted to see if my scissors would cut my shirt."

I tried to hold back a laugh. "Well, what did you learn?"

He took a big sigh. "It definitely cuts it."

"I think it does too. Thank you for coming to me and telling me." I gave him a high five. "And now that we know that it does, let's not do that again, yeah?"

He replied with a smile, "Yeah."

When someone approaches you with their own difficult conversation, something that they know will upset you or hurt you, how you react can determine if they ever come to you in a difficult moment again. Creating space for difficult conversations begins with how you first receive the information. Here are some phrases that will help you make sure that you create a safe space from the start:

- "I'm glad you came to me with this."

You're conveying that you acknowledge that they have a choice in whom to trust and share information with. By showing gratitude and appreciation for their choice to come to you, you allow them to connect to you.

- "Thank you for telling me."

This response acknowledges the effort that it took to come to you, that you understand that sometimes it's not easy to open up and share things.

- "I appreciate your perspective."

No matter what side of an issue they're on, somebody's point of view informs you of a view you might not have had.

Difficult conversations, despite the label, are your

greatest opportunity to connect to another person. Encountering struggle, and overcoming that struggle, brings you closer together, which deepens and strengthens connection. Phrases like the following, however, can have the opposite effect:

- "I know what you're going through."
- "I had a hard day too."
- "Something like that happened to me once."

There's the tendency to give these kinds of statements as a way to relate to the other person, to create connection. More often than not, however, what you're really doing is turning the spotlight on yourself. You've closed off their chance to share, to vent, to express their frustrations. Turning the conversation toward you, even if spoken from a good place, operates to **break** connection. Rather than immediately changing the subject toward something about you, try this method:

1. Ask one question. You can ask more, of course, but just one question will make all the difference. It can be a softball question, like "How are you feeling about that?" or "What are your thoughts about it?" These are open-ended questions that keep the spotlight on the other person and allow them to continue the connection.

2. If you still feel that something you have to say is worth sharing, ask permission. It can be as simple as "Do you mind if I share something with you?" Because you've already shown interest in step one by asking for more from them, they'll likely say yes and be more open to what you have to say.

3. Rather than telling someone what they should do, or what you would do if you were in their shoes, ask, "Can I tell you what I've learned?" People are much more receptive to hearing what you've learned from your own experiences instead of feeling like you're trying to boss them around or sound like a know-it-all.

When someone opens up to you with a difficult conversation of their own, be a safe place. That doesn't mean you have to be happy and positive. That's dishonest. It means only that they need to feel safe and secure enough to communicate with you without fear.

You don't have to pretend that difficult conversations are going to be easy. As you know from chapter one, it's the difficult conversations and conflicts that provide opportunities to improve your relationships. Difficulty is going to happen. Accept it. Welcome it. The deeper the relationship you want to have with someone, the deeper the tolerance you must have for difficult conversation.

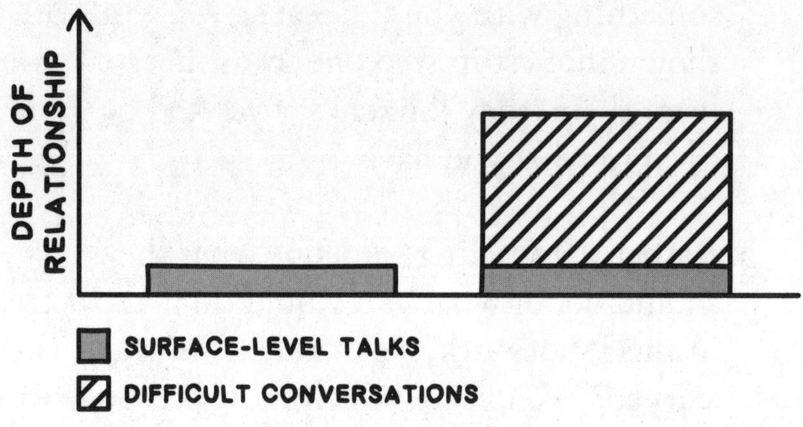

The key is to use the conversations to build connection. By following these methods, you can remove the difficulty before you even begin speaking. Be proactive. Ask the other person for a time and place to have the hard talk. When the conversation begins, drop the pleasantries and get to the heart of the matter right away. Lead with your takeaway to avoid confusion and be clear about the outcome you're seeking. And when the shoe is on the other foot, and the other person needs to have a difficult talk with you, be the person you wish someone would be for you. Be a safe space.

When used wisely, these steps can help you turn your next conversation into an opportunity for connection.

CHAPTER SUMMARY

- The best time to remove the difficult from a difficult conversation is before it even starts.

- When you need to discuss a tough or sensitive subject, set aside dedicated, undistracted time to talk with the other person. Don't push the conversation for the convenience of your own time frame.

- Resist initiating with pleasantries that skirt around the issue at hand, which can be perceived as disingenuous. Instead, be direct. Being direct is kind and maintains your credibility. To do that, lead with your conclusion, the main takeaway.

- Difficult conversations, despite the label, are your greatest opportunity to connect to the other person. Encountering struggle, and overcoming that struggle, brings you closer together, which deepens and strengthens connection.

Afterword

Walking up the cold granite steps leading to the old Texas courthouse, I turned down the long hallway and pushed open the large wooden swinging doors into the courtroom. As I entered, I paused slightly to run through a mental checklist as I scanned the room.

There, behind the bench, was the judge, loudly telling a story to the bailiff and court reporter. Good. Off to the side of the room stood my three opposing attorneys, whispering to each other. Good. Behind my counsel table with my notes and files was my client's chair.

It was empty. Not good.

My head swiveled. Where was my client? I called out to the judge and asked if I could have five minutes before we began. Catching his eye as he nodded, I pushed open the swinging doors again. All that could be heard was the echo of my dress shoes click-clacking on the hard marble floor through the halls as I began my search.

My client's name was Clemon Lee. And Clemon Lee didn't have a cell phone. A sixty-one-year-old elementary school janitor, his life was a routine that did not welcome change. His house phone suited him just fine. I rang the number. Nothing. I started to feel frantic.

Finally, as I rounded my third set of hallways, I saw him, sitting on a bench at the far end of the hall. I slowed my walk and spoke out to him, smiling.

"Mr. Lee? We doing okay?" He didn't respond.

With his legs crossed and arms folded, he held his gaze downward. He wore an old tan suit with a maroon tie. His white shirt was more yellow. I knew from prior conversations with him that this was his church suit. And it was the only suit he owned.

I repeated as I began to sit down next to him, "How are we doing?" We were now shoulder-to-shoulder.

After a moment, he softly said, "They ain't gonna like me."

"What do you mean?" I asked.

"I don't talk good. They're gonna put words in my mouth. I ain't meant for this," he said. He looked understandably worried.

It's normal to be nervous in a courtroom. Twelve jurors watch your every move, a judge in a black robe looks down at you, and an attorney paid by the other side sits eager to cross-examine your credibility.

"Look at my eyes, Clemon. Do I look nervous?" I asked. He slowly shook his head no.

"Have you done anything wrong?" Again, he shook his head no.

And he hadn't. The other driver had hit him. The liability was undisputed. Still, the truth of the facts and the self-consciousness of the mind are two very different things.

"Then okay," I said. "Let's go over it again."

We went over his quick-scan steps to use before going on the stand or when he needed a break to keep his emotions in check. We did a practice round of using conversational breaths to calm his mind before giving an answer into the witness stand microphone. What he needed most of all was to feel confident. Assurance that who the jury would see would be someone not trying to be anyone other than who they were.

We had come up with some short phrases in the months leading up to trial to prepare him for this very moment.

"When you're up on the stand, who will you be?" I quizzed him, starting to stand up.

"Only be Clemon Lee," he answered as he uncrossed his arms and stood up beside me.

I smiled. "That's right. And if the other attorney tries to disagree with you, what does that give you the chance to do?"

"Teach them," he replied as we started walking back toward the courtroom.

"Exactly," I replied. "And when you're not sure how to respond, what will you say first?"

With a wide grin, he responded just as we had rehearsed, "My breath."

"Better?" I asked.

He replied confidently, "Yep, I got this."

Putting my hand on his shoulder, I pushed open the wooden swinging doors into the courtroom one more time.

Here's the part where I have to let you go through your own door.

Like Clemon Lee said, you got this.

You really do.

Over the course of this book, you haven't just learned what to say. You've learned **how** to say it. You've learned different ways to see the communication happening around you. That means you're going to start hearing things differently than you did before. You're going to read others' texts and emails and notice the words, phrases, and fillers that clutter their message. You're going to be more intentional and clear-minded with your words.

You'll also find yourself feeling a greater sense of calm and strength the next time an argument appears. That isn't by happenstance. You've set it there with method and practice, applying the lessons from these twelve chapters. By using a function that shows you how to **say it with control**, **say it with confidence**, and **say it to connect**, you now have a set of tools and strategies that can help you encounter any conflict.

I'll end with how we began. Who do your words say you are? My prayer for you is that you let what you say and how you say it become your family's inheritance. A legacy of who you want to be and how you want to be remembered. A new life. A new you.

Go make your next conversation the one that changes everything.

The 47-Second Version

In the spirit of how I got here, if I had to condense these pages to a forty-seven-second video to post on social media for you, it would sound something like this:

Number one: Never win an argument, or you'll lose a lot more than you gain. When you regulate your reactions before responding, you keep a clear head and a calm mind.

Number two: Confidence isn't an act, it's an outcome. Use words and short phrases that assert your needs and protect your values without fear of disappointment. When you embrace your assertive voice, you make a pathway for more positive change in your life.

Number three: Don't worry yourself over how to change an entire relationship. Focus on changing the next conversation. When you frame a conversation as something to learn, rather than something to prove, you take out the difficulty in building connection.

So try that and follow me.

The Next Steps

I can't thank you enough for reading my book. If you follow me on social media and you're here—hi again, it's still me. Thank you for asking for this book. Thank you for believing in my work and this message for a better world.

So you're ready for your next conversation. What about the next steps?

I want you to go to:

thenextconversation.com/newsletter

If you enjoyed **The Next Conversation**, my stories and takeaways, then you'll like my free newsletter, in which I share one easy, practical communication tip to jump-start your week. You'll also be the first to know about any new projects and writings, and you'll gain early access to any events where I'll be speaking. If you're looking for a next step, this is the first one to take.

And if you'd like to take two steps, you're always welcome in my online community. There you'll find a searchable library of my content filled with on-demand videos, downloadable scripts, and live classes. Go to:

thenextconversation.com/member

Attorney-Client Privilege: Narcissists and Gaslighting

No, this isn't a true attorney-client relationship, and it isn't legally privileged communication. But there is some confidential advice that I wanted to reserve for those who truly need it: how to handle narcissists and gaslighting. It's some of my most sought-after online content, and for good reason. These types of personalities and behaviors are toxic, and knowing what to say when you're on the receiving end of them can often mean the difference between sanity and losing your mind.

That's why I created a hidden bonus chapter on the communication tools you'll need to stand your ground the next time you find yourself under attack.

You can download the chapter in full here: **thenextconversation.com/bonuschapter**

Acknowledgments

So much wouldn't exist without Sierra.

You haven't met her yet, but she's there. Behind every page you've now read, every video and speaking engagement, there's been a sacrifice by my wife to do more than her share of parenting our two young children. She'd say it's nothing. I know it isn't. Any parent knows it isn't. Sierra is also an attorney and has a successful career of her own. Still, she somehow does it all. And if she hadn't taken it on so that I could share this message, none of this would be here, let alone this book.

I consider myself a nice, solid Windows 98–quality product, but a little slower on the output. Sierra is the latest Apple MacBook Pro with a blazing processor chip. She thinks ten times my speed. Do we argue? Absolutely. Do we have the same communication struggles as any other couple? You bet. And for the past decade, believe me, I'm better for it. She's shaped me as much as anyone. When I first started posting the videos, we agreed to keep her and the kids out of social media. She may be in the background, but Sierra is my first sounding board and support.

Just know that whatever I am, she's better.

I also want to acknowledge my parents, David and Sherlyn, not only for how they raised me but also for who they are and the light they bring to the people lucky enough to know them. Thank you, God, for your goodness and hearing my parents' prayer for wisdom and discernment over my life. Let the words of this book lead people to see more of You and less of me.

I'm thankful for the support of my family and friends. To my siblings for making me feel like I walked on the moon and still calling me Bubba. I'm grateful for my best friend, Matt, who kept me steady when I felt overwhelmed during these big life changes. For my mother-in-law, Sunee, whose one-on-one talks never ended without imparting a lesson. And for my Fisher Firm family, especially Liz, whose support and patience have meant the world to me.

I also want to acknowledge and show gratitude for my Civility team who, without hesitation, jumped in headfirst to help me bring this business and mission to life. I'm indebted to their support, enthusiasm, and confidence.

When my followers first began asking for a book, I had no idea where to start. Thankfully, God placed some wonderful people in my path to help me bring this message to you.

Tess Callero, my literary agent, who's been nothing short of wonderful while showing me the ropes of traditional publishing. She has passion and intellect in spades. If you've ever doubted the power of a cold email, this book is living proof.

Jacob Surpin, my editor at TarcherPerigee, and Pippa Wright, my UK editor, for trusting and encouraging me to keep my writing authentic to my voice. Thank you to the entire team at Penguin Random House, including Lota Erinne, Lindsay Gordon, Farin Schlussel, Neda Dallal, Katie Macleod-English, Casey Maloney, Lillian Ball, and Viviana Moreno, and to Megan Newman, Tracy Behar, and Marian Lizzi for being my champions for this book since day one.

Blake Atwood, my book coach, who drove down to spend a week with me, came to my home and had dinner with my family, to make sure that readers would hear my heart in the structure of the pages. When I rolled up my sleeves, he rolled up his.

To Janis Ozolins, who breathed life and character into each chapter's themes with his brilliant illustrations.

To Pete Garceau, for the awesome design on the cover of this book.

And finally, to Jett and Ruby.

One day, when you read this book for the first time, I want you to know that nothing in the world compares to the joy of being your dad. I love you.

Notes

Chapter 4: Control Yourself

82 **scan Grace's body:** Laurie K. McCorry, "Physiology of the Autonomic Nervous System," **American Journal of Pharmaceutical Education** 71, no. 4 (2007): 78.

82 **putting her into fight-or-flight mode:** "Understanding the Stress Response," Harvard Health Publishing, April 3, 2024, https://www.health.harvard.edu/staying-healthy/understanding-the-stress-response.

83 **area of the brain used for higher-order thinking:** Amy F. T. Arnsten, "Stress Signalling Pathways That Impair Prefrontal Cortex Structure and Function," **Nature Reviews Neuroscience** 10, no. 6 (2009): 410–22, https://doi.org/10.1038/nrn2648.

88 **strong, negative reaction in you:** The discussion of triggers in this chapter does not refer to the more clinical definition of "trauma triggers," which specifically refers to something that evokes or recalls a past trauma through sight, sound, or other stimuli. It instead addresses the more general term used in communication to describe words that provoke a strong emotional response, often leading to escalation or intense reactions.

88 **personality and childhood:** For an in-depth discussion on the stress triggers of children and parenting

strategies, I recommend clinical psychologist Dr. Becky Kennedy's book, **Good Inside.**

88 potential dangers to your physical well-being: Brianna Chu et al., "Physiology, Stress Reaction," StatPearls, May 7, 2024, https://pubmed.ncbi.nlm.nih.gov/31082164.

90 you care about what others think: Maayan Katzir and Tal Eyal, "When Stepping Outside the Self Is Not Enough: A Self-Distanced Perspective Reduces the Experience of Basic but Not of Self-Conscious Emotions," **Journal of Experimental Social Psychology** 49, no. 6 (2013): 1089–92, https://doi.org/10.1016/j.jesp.2013.07.006; Jessica L. Tracy and Richard W. Robins, "Putting the Self into Self-Conscious Emotions: A Theoretical Model," **Psychological Inquiry** 15, no. 2 (2004): 103–25, https://doi.org/10.1207/s15327965pli1502_01.

91 personal identity is about how you perceive yourself: Chu-Hsiang (Daisy) Chang et al., "Core Self-Evaluations: A Review and Evaluation of the Literature," **Journal of Management** 38, no. 1 (2011): 81–128, https://doi.org/10.1177/0149206311419661.

91 competence, autonomy, purpose, or values: Richard M. Ryan and Maarten Vansteenkiste, "Self-Determination Theory: Metatheory, Methods, and Meaning," in **The Oxford Handbook of Self-Determination Theory**, ed. Richard M. Ryan (Oxford University Press, 2023), 3–30; Jon L. Pierce and Donald G. Gardner, "Self-Esteem Within the Work and Organizational Context: A Review of the Organization-Based Self-Esteem Literature," **Journal of Management** 30, no. 5 (2004): 591–622, https://doi.org

/10.1016/j.jm.2003.10.001; Steven Hitlin, "Values as the Core of Personal Identity: Drawing Links Between Two Theories of Self," **Social Psychology Quarterly** 66, no. 2 (2003): 118–37, https://doi.org/10.2307/1519843.

93 Loss is the fear of losing: John H. Harvey and Eric D. Miller, "Toward a Psychology of Loss," **Psychological Science** 9, no. 6 (1998): 429–34, https://doi.org/10.1111/1467-9280.00081.

Chapter 5: Control the Moment

101 In arguments, your breath: Alan Fogel, "Waiting to Exhale," **Psychology Today**, September 27, 2010, https://www.psychologytoday.com/ca/blog/body-sense/201009/waiting-to-exhale.

101 very structure of your nasal passages: Carolyn Farnsworth, "What to Know About Nose Breathing vs. Mouth Breathing," **Medical News Today**, November 20, 2023, https://www.medicalnewstoday.com/articles/nose-breathing-vs-mouth-breathing.

106 physiological sigh: Also known as cyclic sighing, a technique popularized by Dr. Andrew Huberman and his podcast, **Huberman Lab**. I recommend the episodes "Tools for Managing Stress & Anxiety" (March 2021) and "How to Breathe Correctly for Optimal Health, Mood, Learning & Performance" (February 2023). For the data, see Melis Yilmaz Balban et al., "Brief Structured Respiration Practices Enhance Mood and Reduce Physiological Arousal," **Cell Reports Medicine** 4, no. 1 (2023): 100895, https://doi.org/10.1016/j.xcrm

.2022.100895; and Deni Ellis Béchard, "The Huberman Effect," **Stanford Magazine**, July 2023, https://stanfordmag.org/contents/the-huberman-effect.

107 "tactical breathing": Noma Nazish, "How to De-Stress in 5 Minutes or Less, According to a Navy SEAL," **Forbes**, December 10, 2021, https://www.forbes.com/sites/nomanazish/2019/05/30/how-to-de-stress-in-5-minutes-or-less-according-to-a-navy-seal/.

107 Box breathing: Samantha K. Norelli, Ashley Long, and Jeffrey M. Krepps, "Relaxation Techniques," StatPearls, August 28, 2023, https://www.ncbi.nlm.nih.gov/books/NBK513238/.

107 benefit of rhythmic breathing: Marc A. Russo, Danielle M. Santarelli, and Dean O'Rourke, "The Physiological Effects of Slow Breathing in the Healthy Human," **Breathe** 13, no. 4 (2017): 298–309, https://doi.org/10.1183/20734735.009817.

116 significantly influences your emotions: Kristen A. Lindquist, Jennifer K. MacCormack, and Holly Shablack, "The Role of Language in Emotion: Predictions from Psychological Constructionism," **Frontiers in Psychology** 6 (2015): 444, https://doi.org/10.3389/fpsyg.2015.00444.

Chapter 7: Assertive Voice

169 Eye contact is another vital component: Joylin M. Droney and Charles I. Brooks, "Attributions of Self-Esteem as a Function of Duration of Eye Contact," **Journal of Social Psychology** 133, no. 5 (1993): 715–22, https://doi.org/10.1080/00224545.1993.9713927.

170 Cadence, the rhythm and pace: William T.

O'Donohue and Jane E. Fisher, eds., **Cognitive Behavior Therapy: Applying Empirically Supported Techniques in Your Practice**, 2nd ed. (John Wiley & Sons, 2008), 27.

Chapter 8: Difficult People

177 **"feel-good hormone"**: Cleveland Clinic, "Dopamine," March 23, 2022, https://my.clevelandclinic.org/health/articles/22581-dopamine.

Chapter 9: Boundaries

210 Boundaries also help you prevent burnout and resentment: Devin J. Rapp, J. Matthew Hughey, and Glen E. Kreiner, "Boundary Work as a Buffer Against Burnout: Evidence from Healthcare Workers During the COVID-19 Pandemic," **Journal of Applied Psychology** 106, no. 8 (2021): 1169–87, https://doi.org/10.1037/apl0000951.

Chapter 10: Frames

224 fewer choices can lead to better outcomes: Barry Schwartz, **The Paradox of Choice: Why More Is Less** (Harper Perennial, 2005), 144.

Chapter 11: Defensiveness

246 cognitive dissonance: Eddie Harmon-Jones and Judson Mills, "An Introduction to Cognitive Dissonance Theory and an Overview of Current Perspectives on the Theory," in **Cognitive Dissonance: Reexamining a Pivotal Theory in Psychology**, 2nd ed., ed. Eddie Harmon-Jones (American Psychological Association, 2019), 3–24, http://www.jstor.org/stable/j.ctv1chs6tk.7.

249 fundamental attribution error: Jessica Koehler, "Decoding the Fundamental Attribution Error," **Psychology Today**, March 27, 2023, https://www.psychologytoday.com/us/blog/beyond-school-walls/202303/decoding-the-fundamental-attribution-error. While academics may differ on the certainty of the concept, I take no side in the debate. What I do know, however, is that the effects of the phenom-enon are sure to influence your communication.
252 confirmation bias: Raymond S. Nickerson, "Confirmation Bias: A Ubiquitous Phenomenon in Many Guises," **Review of General Psychology** 2, no. 2 (1998): 175–220, https://doi.org/10.1037/1089-2680.2.2.175.

Chapter 12: Difficult Conversations

270 good at reading nonverbal cues: Anna Esposito, "The Amount of Information on Emotional States Conveyed by the Verbal and Nonverbal Channels: Some Perceptual Data," in **Progress in Nonlinear Speech Processing**, eds. Yannis Stylianou, Marcos Faundez-Zanuy, and Anna Eposito (Springer-Verlag, 2007), 249–68, https://doi.org/10.1007/978-3-540-71505-4_13.
271 what kind of conversation: In **Never Split the Difference**, by Chris Voss and Tahl Raz, these statements are referred to as "accusation audits." I recommend this book for another great example of handling sensitive conversations and tactical empathy.

Index

Note: Boldface page numbers indicate material in photographs or illustrations.

About the Author

JEFFERSON FISHER is a trial lawyer, writer, and speaker whose work to help people communicate during life's everyday arguments and conversations, with his practical videos and authentic presence, has gained millions of followers around the world, including celebrities and global leaders. He is a sought-after speaker on communication at Fortune 500 companies and government agencies, and hundreds of thousands of people subscribe to his actionable email newsletter and podcast. Fisher is a Texas board-certified personal injury attorney and the founder of Fisher Firm, where he helps people all over the United States connect to trusted legal services. He lives with his wife and two children near Beaumont, Texas.

jeffersonfisher.com
Facebook JustAskJefferson
Instagram Jefferson_Fisher
YouTube JeffersonFisher